THE FERGUSON BROTHERS LYNCHINGS ON LONG ISLAND

6/30/24

THE FERGUSON BROTHERS LYNCHINGS ON LONG ISLAND

A CIVIL RIGHTS CATALYST

CHRISTOPHER VERGA

THE History PRESS

Published by The History Press
Charleston, SC
www.historypress.com

First published 2022

Manufactured in the United States

ISBN 9781467150712

Library of Congress Control Number: 2022939486

In memory of Wilfred Ferguson.

Thank you for sharing your story with me.
May this book bring your family a step closer to closure.

CONTENTS

ACKNOWLEDGMENTS

No one person can own or monopolize the history they write or interpret. The gatekeeper to our history lies in the collective efforts of a community to keep it alive. Who we recognize as heroes or villains is defined by their impacts on the communities they represent. The history of civil rights on Long Island consists of multiple layers, and town and county historical societies and local libraries have encapsulated this history for generations to come.

This book would not have been possible without the help and support of the many people who tirelessly work to preserve this history through image collections and interviews. Thanks to Regina Feeney and Freeport Library's image collection and digitized interviews. I want to thank Karl Grossman for helping through this book's start and finish. Thank you, Jacqueline Green, Lorna Luniewski, and Charmaine McCants-Collins, for helping me work through the book's structuring. Thanks to Eric Nadler and Bob Coen for your assistance and direction for this project. I want to express my gratitude to Lou Carvell for collaborating on research related to February 5, 1946. Special thanks to the University of Rochester's Thomas Dewey Archives and the Woody Guthrie Archives. I would like to express my gratitude for the images of the Tuskegee Airmen and access to other local Long Island history documents provided to me by Dr. Geri Solomon and Hofstra University Special Collections. These images and documents were the backbones of my retelling of an almost forgotten history. I want to extend special recognition to all the local historians I consulted with at the Bay Shore Historical Society, Nassau County Historical Services, and Suffolk County Historical Society. Thanks to Sandi Brewster and Julius Pearse for helping me out with the family genealogies of the Jackson and Ferguson families.

Most of all, I would like to thank Carlo Gibbons for his help in putting me in contact with descendants of the Ferguson family and the FBI documents and, most of all, for providing the idea to make this project happen.

INTRODUCTION

Five Black men stand lined up against a wall in the early morning hours, with a rookie white cop pointing his gun at them, waiting for backup. The five men stand with hands up, scared and shivering in the early cold hours, hoping for a resolution that would not involve the officer firing his gun. Words are exchanged with one of the five men, who was home after a long deployment, still wearing his military uniform proudly, with the traumas of combat hanging on each of his words. Despite the twenty-degree weather, the officer is breaking out in a nervous sweat and regretting how he possibly escalated the situation by cursing the man in the military uniform for giving him an attitude and kicking him before unsheathing his gun.

As the seconds turn into minutes for the officer, the man with the army uniform drops his hands and says something. The officer thinks he said, "I have a forty-five," but the blistery eighteen-mile-per-hour winds blur the words. The officer's heart races, and he squeezes the first shot out from his police-issued .38. The shot echoes off the walls, and the man in the military uniform falls to the ground. One of the other men moves out of fear and nervousness. The officer's gun blares out a second dull cracking shot. The bullet goes through the shoulder of one of the men. After the bullet rips through him, it goes into the head of the shortest of the five. Shrieks of terror become silenced by the officer's overacting adrenaline. No gun was ever recovered from the crime scene. All five of the Black men were unarmed. Despite these facts, long-standing racial tensions between the police department blur the night's events in various eyewitness accounts.

Many in the surrounding Black communities would view this event as a modern lynching or a relic of past lynchings. Some, unaware of the experiences of the Black community, would refer to it as an arrest gone wrong. Others with long-standing views of white supremacy would say that the officer used necessary force.

While those gunshots might have been isolated to this specific corner of the United States, they were heard throughout the country. "Unarmed Black Men Shot and Killed by an Officer" would be the headline in newspapers across the country, setting off a nationwide protest that would last for months. Dozens of civil rights groups descended on the town, which bore the scars of the fatal shooting. Like the national divide along racial lines, the locals chose to support the calls for justice or solidarity for law enforcement. Elected officials also would take one of the two sides, drawing lines for legislative fights and rallying their political base. Social justice activists would argue that structural racism created this event. Movie stars and famous musicians would join pro-justice groups and face public opposition from pro-law enforcement groups that "stand on the side of law and order." Daily mass demonstrations by victim solidarity groups representing various unions or newly formed civil rights groups marched through Manhattan and other cities across America, demanding justice and referring to the events as a modern lynching. These demands evolved into fundraising campaigns to support the work of other social justice groups throughout the country. Pro-law enforcement groups refer to the people marching in the name of justice as "socialists," "Communists," or "un-American." The pro-law enforcement groups would use the American flag at demonstrations to conflate their stance with patriotism. As the protests got louder, the officer was acquitted in the shooting, further frustrating the Black community and fraying any trust of law enforcement.

These events are not coincidental but somewhat ingrained in our collective psyche as a nation. This event did not happen in 2020 or recent decades but on February 5, 1946, in Freeport, New York. Happening at the close of World War II, this event would be one of the catalysts of the 1950s civil rights movement. But the echoes of this seventy-five-year-old event still haunt us today. Keeping this wound fresh is the unfinished work of civil rights activists and the need for long-overdue historical awareness.

Chapter 1
THE FERGUSON AND JACKSON FAMILIES

Charles was born on October 9, 1918, and is rumored to be the only one of the five brothers with a father of Italian ancestry. Charles, Alphonso, Richard, Joseph, and Edward Ferguson (Edward was the oldest of the five) were born to Washington, D.C. native Alma Ferguson. Like many African Americans in the early twentieth century, Alma moved to New York for more job prospects and to escape the relics of slavery in southern states. By 1935, Alma had moved the family to Freeport and later to Bennett Avenue in Roosevelt. Roosevelt was a bedroom community of Freeport Village due to residents in the pre–World War II community sharing the high school and depending on entertainment and shopping within Freeport village limits. The community of Bennington Park in Freeport was an African American and immigrant enclave. Bennington was home to domestic workers, maintenance men, groundskeepers, and porters who maintained the waterfront luxury hotels and operated the local clubs and bars. Bennington Park was a commuter-friendly community, developed initially by Newton Bennington and Charles Powell, between Freeport train tracks and Merrick Road. Powell initially marketed it to middle-class city residents looking for an affordable suburban lifestyle. Within a decade, with the Great Migration of African Americans from the South and an influx of Italian immigration, the community had become predominately Black and Southern Italian.

Hunter Squires, Jackson, American Legion Post No. 1218 in Amityville. *Courtesy of Amityville Historical Society.*

The community built a thriving business district that catered to the needs of the two demographics. This business district would become the leading destination for communities of color. The main strip of stores on Alexander Avenue included The Nest Bar and Grill and a pool hall. A few stores down stood Bobby Joe's Barber Shop (which locals called B and J's) and, on the corner, a candy shop. The candy shop secretly hosted numbers games (an illegal three-digit lottery) for locals.[1] At the center of the Bennington community on Henry Street, a reddish-brown structure with a steeple stood out. This building was the Bethel AME Church, originally built in 1910.

In Roosevelt, neighboring the Ferguson residence, the Jacksons were a local family indigenous to the area; their daughter Minnie would become Charles Ferguson's future wife. Minnie's mother, also named Minnie, was of Shinnecock descent, and her husband, Charles, was of Montaukett heritage. Charles and Minnie had five children, including Minnie, Charles Jr., Bertha, Wilfred, and Louis. Charles, the head of the household, was a laborer who found enough work to support their large family despite the job limitations of the time. The closest Jackson family members were Bill and Myrtle Jackson, who lived in Bellmore. The community of Bellmore was once a historic community of color. But, in the aftermath of urban sprawl, the traditional isolated community was experiencing a change due to higher land prices for development. Most of the Jackson family were cement workers or bricklayers. Minnie's other extended family relocated from eastern Long Island to the surrounding Gilded Age resorts of the nineteenth century for livable wages. For this reason, the Jacksons moved

into Bay Shore, about half an hour east of Freeport. Bay Shore was home to several resort hotels along the Great South Bay. Bay Shore's Courtland House, Linwood, and Prospect House were steps from the ferry terminal to Fire Island's long stretch of ocean beaches, which employed boat builders, hospitality workers, and carpenters. These hotels/resorts kept many families of color gainfully employed. Frederick Fowler Jackson (related to Minnie and a Bay Shore local) enlisted and fought during World War I and served in the legendary Harlem Hell Fighters 360th Regiment. Frederick Jackson fought with French troops at Chateau Thierry and received the highest military honor in France, the Croix de Guerre. Arriving home, he and fellow local Harlem Hell Fighters Arthur Hunter and Arthur Squires became the founding members of the Hunter, Squires, Jackson American Legion Post 1218 in Amityville. But despite the overseas bravery of Frederick and the other local Harlem Hell Fighters, they returned to the same segregated society socially constructed centuries prior.

Frederick Jackson, a descendant of the Montaukett tribe and resident of Bay Shore. Jackson fought in the legendary Harlem Hell Fighters 360th Regiment during World War I. *Courtesy of Sandi Brewster.*

Building a future for her family in Nassau County, Alma Ferguson knew racism was prevalent in the North and New York City's rural areas. But Alma was unaware of the similar system bestowed by the relics of slavery and how it influenced Long Island's twentieth-century life. In contrast to Alma, Minnie and Charles Jackson's families, who were original inhabitants of the region, had a history of fighting the structural confines of slavery for centuries prior. But as the twenty-first century dawned on Long Island, the local native people faced new challenges brought on by the three hundred years of structural racism.

Chapter 2

FIGHTING AGAINST THE RELICS OF SLAVERY

Growing up on Long Island in the 1920s and 1930s, the Fergusons and Jacksons had firsthand account of established racial boundaries, which had their roots in the foundation of Long Island. Like other local native families, the Jacksons' ancestors endured the brunt of European conquest. Relics of a racial caste system were installed in British and Dutch colonial Long Island through enslaved Africans and Native Americans. At its peak, Long Island had the highest slaveholding population among all northern colonies. In Suffolk County, an estimated 18 percent of households enslaved someone, and in Queens (Nassau County was still part of Queens County), 27 percent of households owned an enslaved person. The institution of slavery built generational wealth for the wealthiest families in New York. An enslaved person could be inherited and mortgaged out to expand landholdings. The Gardiner family became an example of generational wealth earned from slavery. The estimated wealth of the family was $134 million in 2004.

Leading up to emancipation in New York State, the long-established town office Overseers of the Poor reenslaved any person freed from bondage under a classification system that deemed them unable to provide for themselves. Overseers of the Poor deeded over the poorest people in the town to the richest as indentured servants for seven years, during which time they would have to prove that they could provide for themselves. Failure would mean a person could be re-indentured for another seven years. The only way to confirm that you could provide for yourself was to either own land or know a trade. In many cases, the persons indentured became stuck in a cycle of servitude much like slavery itself. Attempting to survive within this caste system, many former enslaved people established communities in Native American enclaves. The indigenous Montaukett people, by 1741, had become isolated from other nearby Native American communities due to English colonists enforcing a ban on other natives visiting Montaukett tribal land within East Hampton Montauketts. These traditional community interactions were practiced for thousands of years and were essential for marriages. The Montauketts grew despite the ban on community interaction designed to destroy the population. The Montaukett population's survival was through marriages to local African American people, allowing families of African ancestry to be absorbed into the tribe.[2] But blurring the lines between Black and Native Americans would be used to rob them of their cultural identity and land ownership claims in court by European landowners.[3] Sacred ancestral land that spanned the entire southeast end of Long Island supported the Montaukett Nation for a period estimated at ten thousand years. By the end of the nineteenth century, only a few thousand acres of land remained in Montaukett possession.

Further isolating Black and indigenous communities was the 1821 clause added to the New York State Constitution that required a person to own $100 to $250 worth of property to vote. Despite losing rights to ancestral land and having little to no voice in government, these communities were economically expanding. Families such as the Jacksons made good wages in masonry work for the luxury hotels and resorts that dotted the South Shore of Long Island. Other families of color secured jobs as baymen, harvesting the lucrative oyster beds to feed the growing demands of high-end New York City restaurants. Communities of color also enjoyed leisure activities such as baseball tournaments, which became famous nationally. The establishment of the Cuban Giants in the South Shore community of Babylon Village made the local Argyle Hotel more profitable due to publicized championship games. The Cuban Giants would become the first baseball team established in what became known as the Negro Leagues.

As many communities of color slowly made economic gains, one of the region's first civil rights movements took shape. Soldiers in the "colored units" that fought in the Civil War came home with Reconstruction ideals. Many of these soldiers fought, believing they were ending slavery throughout the country and creating the foundation for an equitable society for all communities of color, local and national. One such soldier returning to civilian life was Charles Devine Brewster of Amityville. Brewster was

Above: The Montaukett tribe of eastern Long Island in the late 1890s. The Jackson family are descendants the Montaukett Nation, who were the original inhabitants of Long Island. *Courtesy of the Library of Congress.*

Left: Roxanna Green Brewster (*left*) and Mary Bunn Green were both of Montaukett descent and settled in Bay Shore. *Courtesy of Sandi Brewster.*

a local native from the Montaukett Nation, who had strong family ties to the Jacksons, and served in the Twentieth Colored Regiment as a private. Brewster and his regiment fought in the Battle of Salem Church, leading to the Battle of Chancellorsville. Once discharged, he returned to his Albany Avenue home in Amityville.

In 1895, there were separate schools for whites and students of color, but a new school used tax revenue collected from both communities. Brewster was outraged that the new school was only for white students and refused his son Irving admission. Organizing other families of color, such as the Treadwells and Mayhews, Brewster petitioned and aired their grievances at the annual school meeting. Brewster requested that the students of color be admitted to the new school, adding, "We are bound to enforce our rights, and no expense will be spared in prosecuting our claims."[4] The school board closed the "colored school" and merged the enrolled students of color with the white students in the newly constructed school to avoid negative attention. Following this win, reported in great depth in the widely circulated newspaper the *Brooklyn Daily Eagle*, other communities of color started taking up similar causes throughout the region. In 1883, the local board of education in Brooklyn passed a rule to abolish racial discrimination, enrolling all students living in the zoned areas of a district. But the 1898 merging of Brooklyn into Greater New York City made Brooklyn and the other boroughs reverse their educational policies.[5] In Queens County, communities of color petitioned that the newly unified board of education had to uphold the 1883 Brooklyn Board of Education's ruling. After twenty-four months of organizing, New York State Governor Theodore Roosevelt (before becoming William McKinley's vice president and president in 1901) issued an executive order to end separate schools of color. These successful efforts came more than fifty years before *Brown v. Board of Education*, aiming to abolish segregated schools and overturning *Plessy v. Ferguson*, which legalized segregation through the "separate but equal" ruling.

Further building on civil rights gains, organized activism took root in established chapters of the Women of Color Social Club. The organization mobilized communities around challenging the relics of slavery and continuing the efforts for people of color to get into the growing middle class. This organization's goals included providing financial assistance for economically struggling people and moral guidance locally. Rising in influence in the 1890s, this group peaked in membership by 1930. Inspired by this organization, Anne Smith, a Shinnecock native, established the Equal Suffrage League. The league's main goal was to get women of color the right to vote. These gains and mobilizing efforts became overshadowed by two devastating events that stalled all progress.

In the fall of 1910, Chief Wyandank, leader of the Montaukett Nation, was engaged in a legal battle with the Benson family over the ownership of the Montauketts' remaining tribal land. The Benson family purchased the land from a member of the tribe, speculating that the expanding Long Island Railroad and other developers would be interested in the vast acreage. The Montaukett tribe argued that the sale was not legal because of a clause in Section 37, Article 1 in the New York State Constitution, which "prohibited the purchase of Indian lands without approval of state legislator." New York State Supreme Court Judge Abel Blackmar presided over the case. Blackmar had to determine if the land purchase was illegal or if the Montaukett Nation should be classified as a tribe with the legal standing for landownership protection under New York State law. Nine years earlier, the *Montoya v. United States* ruling set standards that a tribe was a "body of Indians of the same or similar race, united in a community under one leadership government." The Benson family's lawyer argued the Montaukett tribal sovereignty did not fall within the *Montoya* criteria. In October 1910, Judge Blackmar announced his verdict: "[The] Montauk tribe has disintegrated. They have no internal government and live shiftless lives of hunting, fishing, and cultivating the ground. They often leave Montauk for long periods to work in some menial capacity for whites." That verdict officially ended state recognition of the tribe, revoking more than one hundred years of treaties. The effect of this ruling on the Montauketts would set in motion an appeal or reversal for decades to come.

In March 1913, communities of color across Suffolk and Nassau Counties experienced another devastating blow. The Mayhew family were respected elders in the Montaukett tribe and held leadership roles in many communities of color. Charles Mayhew, a son of one of the elders, was employed in Babylon Village Sherman House stables. The Mayhews and Jacksons had long-standing bonds within the community and were co-workers in the surrounding stables. On March 12, Charles Mayhew drank and fought with a local white man, Arthur Bennett. Bennett filed a complaint against Mayhew later in the day. The incident had no arrest or warrant issued for Mayhew.

Upon hearing the complaint, provisional officer Luke Devin went to the Sherman House stables, where Mayhew was staying. On Saturday at 11:00 p.m., Devin entered the room where Mayhew was sleeping, woke him up, and demanded he come with him. Within three minutes, Mayhew, unarmed, was shot in the chest; he would later die from his wound. The three minutes that led to the shooting would become the center of headlines across Long Island. Officer Devin claimed that he ordered Mayhew to get dressed and come with him, and Mayhew, reportedly drunk, attacked him; Devin took out a second revolver and shot him during a struggle. Mayhew stated, "I was pulled out of bed, and Devin put a chain on me. I resisted because I was not told why I was under arrest and had to get dressed. Once on my feet, Devin shot me and left the room. I had no weapon."[6] The Babylon Village Department suspended Devin pending investigation, but a grand jury acquitted him despite the prosecutor preparing charges for manslaughter. Although many town officials questioned Devin's actions, he remained with the department until 1915. This case of abusive police power became part of a collection of setbacks in racial equality, although the decade of the 1920s would see further backslides.

As the movement for progress in equality stalled, Long Island's landscape evolved rapidly. Developments in Nassau County slowly started transforming local town governments through a sharp shift in demographics. Nassau County's population increased from 83,930 in 1910 to 126,120 by 1920. This 51 percent increase was partially due to African Americans leaving the South or New York City limits for more economic opportunities and Catholic immigrants migrating from southern Europe. The population growth would come with fierce resistance from locals forming chapters of the most prominent white supremacist group of the era, the Ku Klux Klan. The Klan's influence in local communities throughout Long Island further segregated housing developments. In the early 1930s, Alma Ferguson and her family, moving into Long Island, quickly learned to recognize the invisible and visible lines enforced by the Klan—from its annual solidarity parades to elected officials' open acceptance of Klan endorsements.

Chapter 3

INVISIBLE AND VISIBLE LINES OF SEGREGATION

The most visible aspect of segregation that Charles, Alphonso, Richard, Joseph, and Edward faced growing up was the rise of the Ku Klux Klan. Relics of a racial caste system that originated in the colonial era led to Klan ideology in the 1920s and 1930s. The Klan on Long Island fought against any form of racial integration and intimidated new immigrant groups with their ability to consolidate political power. The resurgence of the Klan spread in part through the pro-Klan movie *The Birth of a Nation*. Almost every downtown theater across Long Island played the movie, escalating locals' interest in the Klan. The New York Klan targeted not only people of color but Jewish and Catholic communities as well. A 39 percent increase in the Catholic demographic had the largest impact in New York City and the surrounding areas between 1900 and 1920, totaling 1,325,000 people. The Catholic Diocese comprised Long Island's Kings, Queens, Nassau, and Suffolk Counties, which grew at the fastest rate of 40 percent in 1920 to 800,000. The rise in Catholicism came with a decrease in Protestantism. In 1900, Protestants comprised 47.40 percent of New York City and the surrounding metropolitan area. The 47.40 percent dropped to 34.55 percent in New York City and the surrounding metro area within ten years.

With the growth of Catholic and African American populations and the rise of Prohibition, the Klan boosted its recruitment by distributing various fake news periodicals to generate anxiety and fear over the changing demographics. Circulation of Klan-based newspapers grew throughout the

Top: The Klan at a church in St. James attempting to recruit new members. *Courtesy of Smithtown Historical Society*.

Bottom: The Klan initiating female members on Long Island. *Courtesy of the Library of Congress*.

county, and local newspapers such as the *Freeport News* limited their coverage of the Klan. Newspapers criticizing Klan community influence included the *Brooklyn Daily Eagle*, the *New York Times*, and *The Tablet*, a Catholic-based newspaper. Two of the most widely circulated periodicals in Nassau, Suffolk, and Queens Counties in the late 1920s were the Klan-based newspaper *Vigilance* and *Kourier* magazine. *Kourier* magazine, in July 1927, declared that

This page: The Klan having an annual parade/rally in Patchogue, Long Island. *Courtesy of Longwood Library*.

the "Catholic church teaches disloyalty to America and electing Catholic Governor Alfred Smith will purposely promote the breakdown of America and its values."[7] One edition of *Vigilance* stated that "Catholics accumulated weapons in the columns of their Churches and were conspiring to commit random acts of terrorism." In addition to the fake news, Klan chapters sponsored town hall meetings defending their bigotry. A woman who claimed to be a former nun addressed the crowd about how she supposedly endured slavery from the church and how the Catholics preyed on trustful Protestants.[8] During the same town hall meeting, the Klan preached that Nassau and Suffolk Protestant communities were under attack by Catholic-affiliated organizations, such as the Knights of Columbus militia, which allegedly swore oaths to wage war against American values.

Local Klan chapters spread rumors that Catholic churches within New York were instituting a boycott against Long Island Protestants.[9] In response to this rumor, the Klan demanded and organized economic boycotts against the Catholic community.

The non-white populations across Long Island faced violent intimidation from local Klan chapters if they did not comply with their imposed racially enforced boundaries. One example of intimidation occurred when the Suffolk

This page: The Klan in a funeral procession in Smithtown. *Courtesy of Smithtown Historical Society.*

County Klan burned down the Catholic church and orphanage Little House of Providence on two separate occasions in 1922. A member of the Brooklyn Diocese, Monsignor Bernard John Quinn, built the church and Black orphanage Little House of Providence (current-day Little Flower Children Services) in Wading River despite threats from locals and Klan members. After his church burned down twice, Quinn rebuilt and advocated against the Klan until he died in 1940. In Nassau County, on February 12, 1923, the Freeport Black community was celebrating the birthday of Lincoln. In response, the

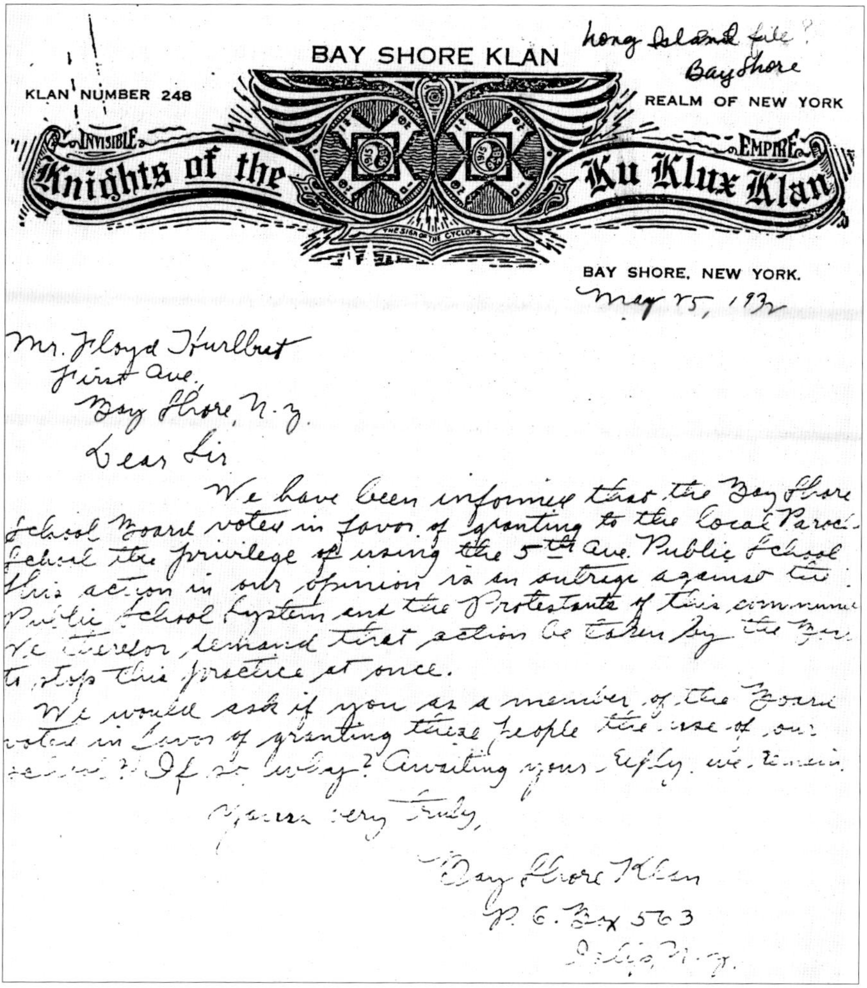

BAY SHORE KLAN

Long Island file? Bay Shore

KLAN NUMBER 248

REALM OF NEW YORK

INVISIBLE EMPIRE

Knights of the Ku Klux Klan

THE SIGN OF THE CYCLOPS

BAY SHORE, NEW YORK.

May 25, 192[illegible]

Mr. Floyd Hurlbut
First Ave.
Bay Shore, N.Y.

Dear Sir

We have been informed that the Bay Shore School Board voted in favor of granting to the local Paroc. School the privilege of using the 5th Ave. Public School. This action in our opinion is an outrage against the Public School System and the Protestants of this community. We therefor demand that action be taken by the Board to stop this practice at once.

We would ask if you as a member of the Board voted in favor of granting these people the use of our school? If so why? Awaiting your reply, we remain

Yours very truly,

Bay Shore Klan
P.O. Box 563
Islip, N.Y.

Letter from the Bay Shore Klan to the local school's administrator, Floyd Herbert. The Klan expressed outrage over having local Catholic groups use the school. *Courtesy of Bay Shore Historical Society.*

Klan burned multiple crosses near the celebration.[10] Following the negative press, representatives of the Klan demanded to speak in Black churches about their racial platform. In Huntington, sixteen Klan members marched into the Huntington AME Church in the middle of the service and told the startled congregation, "They are only against the mixing of white and black blood. The Klan only stood for racial purity, and hostile press had misrepresented them."[11] After the speech, the Klan reminded the congregation lynching was down by 50 percent because of the understanding of racial purity.

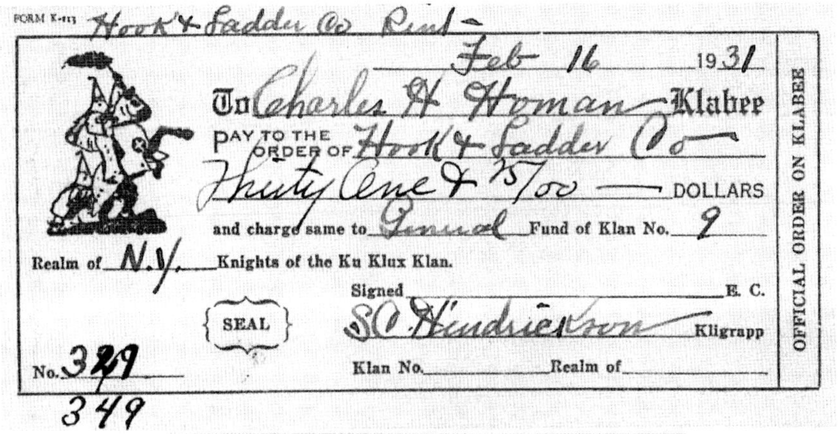

FORM K-113 Hook & Ladder Co Rent

Feb 16 1931

To Charles H Homan Klabee

PAY TO THE ORDER OF Hook & Ladder Co

Thirty One & 75/00 DOLLARS

and charge same to General Fund of Klan No. 9

Realm of N.Y. Knights of the Ku Klux Klan.

Signed E. C.

SEAL

S C Hendrickson Kligrapp

No. 329 349 Klan No. Realm of

OFFICIAL ORDER ON KLABEE

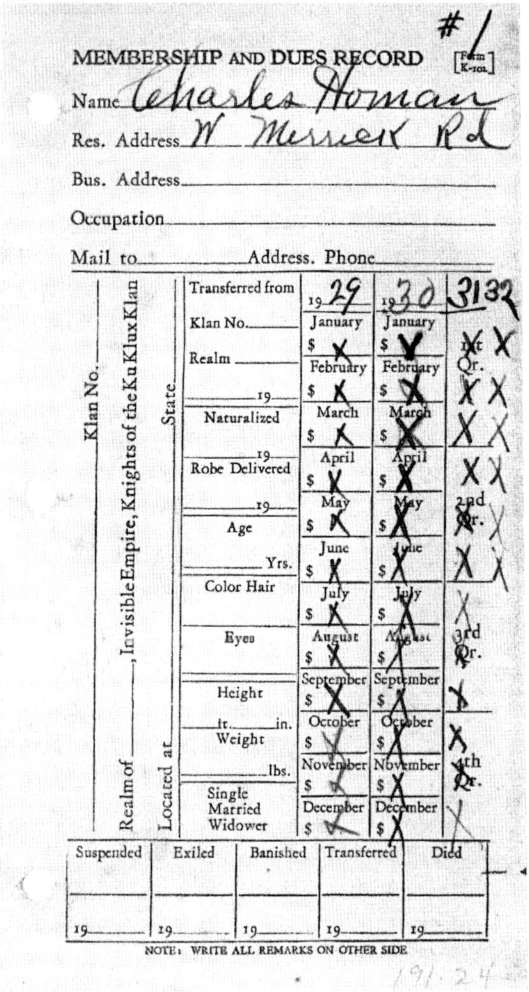

#1

MEMBERSHIP AND DUES RECORD [Form K-101]

Name Charles Homan

Res. Address W Merrick Rd

Bus. Address

Occupation

Mail to Address. Phone

Klan No. , Invisible Empire, Knights of the Ku Klux Klan

Realm of

State

Located at

Transferred from

Klan No.

Realm

19

Naturalized

19

Robe Delivered

19

Age

Yrs.

Color Hair

Eyes

Height

ft. in.

Weight

lbs.

Single
Married
Widower

1929	1930	31	32
January $ X	January $ X	1st Qr. X	X
February $ X	February $ X	X	X
March $ X	March $ X	X	X
April $ X	April $ X	X	X
May $ X	May $ X	2nd Qr. X	X
June $ X	June $ X	X	X
July $ X	July $ X	X	
August $ X	August $ X	3rd Qr.	
September $ X	September $ X	X	
October $ X	October $ X	X	
November $ X	November $ X	4th Qr.	
December $ X	December $ X	X	

Suspended	Exiled	Banished	Transferred	Died
19	19	19	19	19

NOTE: WRITE ALL REMARKS ON OTHER SIDE

191.24

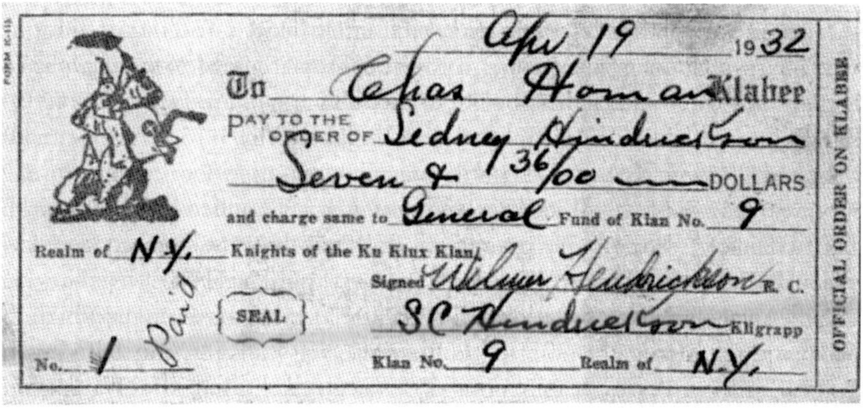
FORM K-113

Apr 19 1932

To Chas Homan Klabee

PAY TO THE ORDER OF Sidney Hendrickson

Seven & 36/00 DOLLARS

and charge same to General Fund of Klan No. 9

Realm of N.Y. Knights of the Ku Klux Klan

Signed Wilmer Hendrickson E. C.

SEAL

S C Hendrickson Kligrapp

No. 1 Paid

Klan No. 9 Realm of N.Y.

OFFICIAL ORDER ON KLABEE

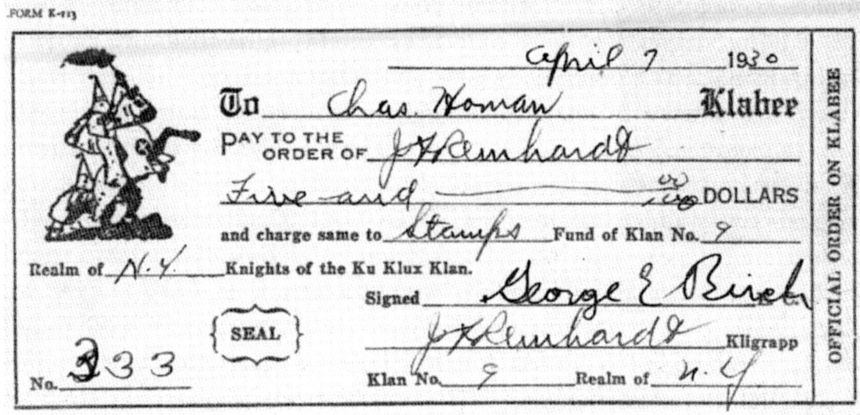
FORM K-113

April 7 1930

To Chas. Homan Klabee

PAY TO THE ORDER OF J H Reinhardt

Five and 00 DOLLARS

and charge same to Stamps Fund of Klan No. 9

Realm of N.Y. Knights of the Ku Klux Klan.

Signed George E Birch E.C.

SEAL

J H Reinhardt Kligrapp

No. 333

Klan No. 9 Realm of N.Y.

OFFICIAL ORDER ON KLABEE

Opposite and above: Receipt of rental hall from a local fire department and paid membership receipts of a local Klan member. *Courtesy of Suffolk County Historical Society.*

In many public recruitment drives, the Klan attempted to distance itself from bigotry directly and stated that it was the defender of religious liberties and democratic institutions. Once someone expressed interest in the Klan, potential members were assigned to read the *Klansmen: Guardian of Liberty*. This book was a question-and-answer guide about the Klan's racial/political platform. One passage declared that "the Klan is not anti-Catholic, anti-Jew, anti-Negro or anti-foreign, it is Pro-Protestant and Pro-American." This "Pro-American" stance was an attempt by the Klan to wallpaper over its white nationalist doctrine.

As Klan membership grew, its political influence expanded from a local to a state level. A political rallying point for the Klan was the 1918 election of Catholic Democratic candidate Al Smith for New York governor. Smith ran against Republican incumbent Charles Whitman, who ran on law and order and other socially conservative issues. Following Smith's two-year term (the New York Constitution of 1938 extended the term to four years), Nathan Miller succeeded him, but within two years, Smith won a second term in the election of 1922. In response to Smith's election wins as governor, the Klan ramped up its grass-roots efforts to take control of the state assembly, senate, and local town offices. The Klan's newsletters circulating in New York City attempted to discredit Smith and his allies based on his Catholic beliefs. An example of this was the November 21, 1924 edition of *Vigilance*, which reported that Al Smith was conspiring to make America a colony of the Roman church. The Republican Party clubs in lower New York had moderate leadership and became the focus of attacks from the extreme wing of their party. One of the state's most prominent Republican clubs in Jamaica, Queens, forced out senior leadership and installed Klan-sympathetic leader John Simpson.[12] In a mass mailing throughout Nassau, Queens, and Suffolk Counties, the Klan listed its endorsement of "full bred American state candidates." The opposite side of the mailing noted the religions of the opposing candidates who were Catholic or Jewish.[13]

The most closely contested election across Long Island was for Islip Town supervisor. Islip Town within Suffolk County had a growing African American and Italian population, which became a bellwether for the following year's local state assembly and senate elections. During the Islip Town elections, the Islip Republican committee issued poll watching certificates to various local Ku Klux Klan chapters. The 1923 elections had Klan-endorsed candidate Frank Rogers defeating James Richardson by just four votes, with all other Klan-backed candidates taking control of all offices across Suffolk County.[14] The 1926 Freeport Village elections had the local Klan openly endorse candidates similar to those in Islip. Running under the Klan-supported party ticket, the Citizens Party, were Washington Vanderpoel (one-time Democrat nominee for village trustee), John Randall, William Gatter, and Fred Patterson. The competing party, the Peoples Ticket, saw Robert Christie, Wallace Young, Samuel Levey, and Fred Booth. This election was a split-ticket win, with two Klan-endorsed candidates elected to village trustee positions with two-year terms. One defeated Klan-backed candidate was Charles Shea, who was added to the ballot last minute to run against Catholic village treasurer George Bird. The last-minute efforts to defeat a Catholic candidate failed, as Bird won 1,142 votes and Shea received only 200.

The Klan parades and rallies across the South Shore towns of Nassau and Suffolk influenced not just local/state politics but commerce. Many

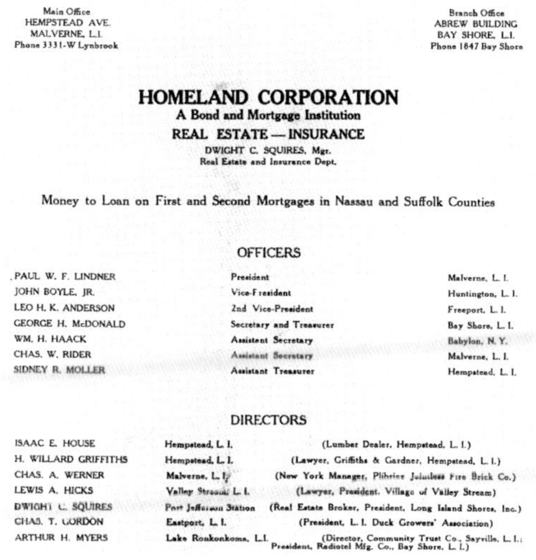

Main Office
HEMPSTEAD AVE.
MALVERNE, L.I.
Phone 3331-W Lynbrook

Branch Office
ABREW BUILDING
BAY SHORE, L.I.
Phone 1847 Bay Shore

HOMELAND CORPORATION
A Bond and Mortgage Institution
REAL ESTATE — INSURANCE
DWIGHT C. SQUIRES, Mgr.
Real Estate and Insurance Dept.

Money to Loan on First and Second Mortgages in Nassau and Suffolk Counties

OFFICERS

PAUL W. F. LINDNER	President	Malverne, L. I.
JOHN BOYLE, JR.	Vice-President	Huntington, L. I.
LEO H. K. ANDERSON	2nd Vice-President	Freeport, L. I.
GEORGE H. McDONALD	Secretary and Treasurer	Bay Shore, L. I.
WM. H. HAACK	Assistent Secretary	Babylon, N. Y.
CHAS. W. RIDER	Assistant Secretary	Malverne, L. I.
SIDNEY R. MOLLER	Assistant Treasurer	Hempstead, L. I.

DIRECTORS

ISAAC E. HOUSE	Hempstead, L. I.	(Lumber Dealer, Hempstead, L. I.)
H. WILLARD GRIFFITHS	Hempstead, L. I.	(Lawyer, Griffiths & Gardner, Hempstead, L. I.)
CHAS. A. WERNER	Malverne, L. I.	(New York Manager, Plibrico Jointless Fire Brick Co.)
LEWIS A. HICKS	Valley Stream, L. I.	(Lawyer, President, Village of Valley Stream)
DWIGHT C. SQUIRES	Port Jefferson Station	(Real Estate Broker, President, Long Island Shores, Inc.)
CHAS. T. GORDON	Eastport, L. I.	(President, L. I. Duck Growers' Association)
ARTHUR H. MYERS	Lake Ronkonkoma, L.I.	(Director, Community Trust Co., Sayville, L. I.; President, Radiotel Mfg. Co., Bay Shore, L. I.)

This page: Pictured is a leaflet from a Klan rally in Mineola, July 3–6, 1926. On the reverse side are the companies that sponsored the rally, including Malverne developer Paul Lindner's mortgage company. *Courtesy of Suffolk County Historical Society.*

local business owners looking to cash in on crowds of Klan rallies showed their support for the Klan by hanging signs in their store windows that read "TWAK" ("Trade only with a Klansman"). This sign reflected Klan solidarity and demonstrated their willingness to hire only white Anglo-Saxon Protestants, centralizing resources and wealth among active Klan and white American-born Protestants. One example of the Klan's influence on local economics was its relationship with Paul Lindner. Lindner was one of the founders of the village of Malverne, president of Malverne Bank and the Homeland Cooperation, which oversaw many mortgages underwritten in Nassau County. Lindner also would sponsor Klan events throughout the county, simultaneously advertising his mortgage services. By the mid-1920s, Klan membership had peaked at an estimated one in seven Long Islanders. As a result, communities of color became more segregated when it came to residential housing and public safety. Directly and indirectly, the Klan used multiple vigilante groups to influence local village police departments to enforce these societal racial barriers, but similar to its political gains, it was a process that relied on fake sensational stories.

Chapter 4

KLAN'S INFLUENCE ON LOCAL LAW ENFORCEMENT AND REFORM

Prohibition enabled the Ku Klux Klan to promote its definition of law and order. The Klan worked with the Anti-Saloon League on a state level to create new laws. These laws targeted various immigrant groups. An example of these laws included banning sacramental wine, which Anti-Saloon League president William Anderson pioneered. Anderson was a firm nativist who promoted prohibition and targeted Catholics as un-American in his speeches. Anderson publicly supported the Klan's platform and claimed it was a natural response to Catholic opposition to prohibition. In addition to influencing state law, the Klan formed vigilante committees that local law officials empowered in many cases.[15] Klan-affiliated vigilante groups such as the Citizens League of Suffolk County and Southside Law Enforcement League went into communities seeking out any possible rumor of gambling dens or rumrunning rings. The targets of the Klan and other vigilante groups included communities of color, new immigrants, Jewish people, and Catholics. In the early morning hours, it was not uncommon for establishments neighboring Freeport's Bennington Park to have a twenty-five-foot cross lit on fire and a sign nailed to the front door that read, "Beware: the eye of the Klan is on you."

The Freeport Klan's reported vigilantism made headlines throughout the state in late August 1924. In a local drugstore on Atlantic Avenue, manager Ernest Louis faced accusations of aggressively grabbing thirteen-year-old Dorothy Shedlock by her arm and kissing her while she was shopping with her fourteen-year-old friend Hazel Rasmus. The incident was investigated by Freeport police, which found no evidence of Louis's actions. The Nassau County District Attorney's Office further investigated the event, saw no basis for the accusation, and dismissed any potential charges. Louis, who was Jewish, attracted the attention of the Klan. The following week, Freeport trustee Milford Van Riper and a group of men walked into the drugstore demanding to see Louis.[16] Once Ernest Louis greeted the men, they told him, "Freeport is not big enough for you and the Klan." The following Tuesday night, Ernest; his wife, Florence; and his brother-in-law, Samuel Schulman, closed the drugstore for the evening and were walking home. Midway on their walk home, a car suddenly stopped in front of the trio, and five Klansmen got out, pushed Florence and Samuel aside, grabbed Ernest, put him in the car, and drove off. The kidnapping happened in front of a village police officer, who did not intervene. In a panic, Florence and Samuel contacted county law enforcement. Once in the car, Ernest recognized one of the Klansmen's voices as a Freeport firefighter, who instructed him to "keep your head down going through the village and no bodily harm will come of you."[17] The kidnappers drove Ernest to Babylon, Westbury, and a Hicksville hotel, where they kept him bound. The kidnappers then had him call his wife and tell her, "I'm all right." At the Hicksville hotel, the Klan warned Ernest that he had one more chance to leave town due to his mistreatment of the young girls.[18] Once they warned him, they asked if he needed money for a cab and left him at the hotel.

The next day, a traumatized Ernest Louis went to Nassau County law enforcement, who then conducted a lineup of suspects who fit the description of kidnappers. With seven men in the lineup, Ernest picked twenty-four-year-old Travis Parker as one of the men. Parker denied involvement in the kidnapping and was held on $1,000 bail. In defiance of the district attorney's investigation, the Klan had a solidarity parade in Freeport. More than two thousand Klan members in full robes but no face coverings marched through the busy intersections of Bayview Avenue and Johnson Place. The Klan had two floats. One float read, "Teach the Bible in Public Schools," the second float had a Klansman statue in full uniform protecting a little girl. Between the floats were several robed Klansmen carrying banners that read, "Protect American Womanhood."[19] But Freeport Chief of Police John Hartman was drawing the most attention, heading the parade and carrying the American flag. Ernest Louis sold his drugstore and left town in the days following the parade. On September 24, Freeport Village Police Court Judge Hilbert Johnson dropped the kidnapping charges against Travis Parker due to Ernest Louis not sufficiently identifying him in the crime.[20]

After the kidnapping, the Klan targeted the Roosevelt family of Arthur Willett for rumored mistreatment of local children. Willett, known in the community for being part of one of the oldest families on Long Island and a descendant of one of the signers of the Declaration of Independence, outraged the local Klan by marrying a Catholic. The Klan mailed him a letter on the local chapter stationery reading:

> *It has come to our notice that you are maliciously harassing and annoying your neighbors. This is to warn you that this practice must stop at once, and if you do not stop, there will not be room for you and the Knights of the Ku-Klux Klan in this County. KNIGHTS OF THE KU-KLUX KLAN. Invisible Realm of New York.*[21]

In response to the Klan's letter and Willett's fear of being kidnapped, county police posted a squad car in front of the home until the threat subsided.

To reform the county police force and break the local Klan vigilantism, Nassau County attempted to unify all local town police forces into a county force. The county police would centralize authority and remove local town authority, providing more accountability. During the 1920s, local police departments such as Freeport were not only influenced by the Klan but also rumored to be corrupted by bribes of organized rumrunners and bootleggers. By the mid-1920s, Nassau County deputy sheriff Charles Hansen and Tyree Bacon, the Rockville Centre police force captain, had been indicted for bootlegging and receiving bribes from organized rumrunners. Following these indictments, a 1924 New York state inquiry order by Governor Al Smith on the impact of Nassau County politics found that Ku Klux Klan was becoming Nassau County's primary influencer in politics and law enforcement.[22] On February 14, 1930, the *Brooklyn Daily Eagle* interviewed Nassau County Police Department spokesman Inspector Frank McCahill, who stated, "The Nassau County Police Department is not interested in politics, nor political organizations. It is the department's interest to detect and prevent crime. But how can a village official with no police experience conduct a police department? When this is done, it creates politics."[23] The argument that advocated separating political organizations and policing became the reasoning for merging several police departments into a unified county-based force. Freeport Village opposed a centralized county policing system and prioritized its local law enforcement to remain separate from the county-based force. After merging several local village forces, the newly formed professional county force would be rocked to its core in 1932.

Freeport police officers posing in from of the station and auto patrol unit. *Courtesy of Freeport Historical Society.*

Nathan Hacker (aka Hyman Stark), a twenty-four-year-old living in Manhattan, was a former army private who became known for his skills as a boxer. Later, following a stint in the army, Stark developed a career in street-level theft. On July 15, Stark and three other men were suspected of breaking into the home of fifty-eight-year-old Valeria Hizinski in Roslyn. The perpetrators held up and assaulted Hizinski and robbed her of the home's valuables. Hizinski was the mother of Nassau County detective Joseph Hizinski, and this act infuriated the detective and his fellow officers. Within hours of the robbery, the four were located and arrested on Northern Boulevard, across from Munson Hill Country Club in Roslyn. Following being taken into custody and an hours-long interrogation, one of the four suspects, Hyman Stark, was transported for medical attention but died from a fractured skull and broken larynx. On July 19, thirteen officers were suspended for either brutality or perjury. Nassau Deputy Chief Frank Tappen was charged with third-degree murder. This murder exposed the police tactics of interrogation. The tactics included placing a foot on the prisoner's throat and stomach, smashing a person across the head with a heavy ledger, multiple cops punching the prisoners, or beatings with rubber hoses.[24] On September 9, following a turbulent, month-long trial, one jury verdict was deadlocked, and a second jury ruled for an acquittal of Tappen and all the other defendant officers. Nonetheless, the county supervisors collectively voted to dismiss Tappen from the county police force. The result of the case and the media's coverage of the brutality slowed the town's mergers into a single county police department.

The Klan's influence in politics and the vigilante-like policing practices persisted and kept communities of color on the defensive. Compounding Klan threats would be the stalled employment growth of the Great Depression. The constant job growth, a point of pride on Long Island, would change in the early 1930s, leaving uncertain futures for hundreds of businesses.

Chapter 5

BOOM AND BUST

Economic Crisis

By the early 1930s, Long Island was facing the worst economic depression in its history. On October 24, 1929, the stock market crashed, and as a result, nine thousand banks failed, and the national unemployment rate peaked at 25 percent. In a short time, all the superficial wealth throughout the state of New York evaporated. The aviation manufacturing industry in the Hempstead Plains soon comprised vacant buildings surrounded by overgrown grass and scrub bushes. Resort-based communities that dotted South Shore towns and villages suffered the most due to little to no demand for weekend getaways. Many vacation homes along South Shore communities faced foreclosure, straining local tax revenues. Locals who worked on large estates for America's wealthiest or toiled in once-popular resorts found themselves unemployed, homeless, and wandering from town to town for work.[25] The western parts of Nassau County and eastern Queens by Thurston's Creek became known as Hungry Harbor due to the squatter shacks erected by locals who lost their homes.[26] Many homeless residents of New York City migrated to Nassau and Suffolk farms to seek employment. Dozens of hungry people dug through harvested potato fields to see if any small potatoes had been left behind.[27] Most affected by the economic devastation were communities of color, which relied on luxury spending of resorts, horse farms, or the maintenance of estates.

By 1934, more than $9 million was allocated for relief in Nassau County municipalities (an estimated $20 million today). But the federal economic relief did very little to aid local villages and towns. Further contributing to economic problems, family farms, which for generations contributed to the local economy, broke down into systems of community bartering. With lower tax revenues, local villages and towns such as Hempstead, Glen Cove, and Long Beach could not make payroll for their employees. With all the economic woes of the region, progressive governor and future president Franklin Roosevelt kept shovel-ready state public works projects flowing. The Meadowbrook, Grand Central, Southern and Northern State Parkways, and Triborough Bridge created jobs for many Long Islanders. By the early 1930s, President Roosevelt had extended his New Deal programs into every Long Island village and town. Freeport locals were hired to paint the Freeport Post Office murals and construct the newly designed Freeport Sewage Disposal Plant. Despite the federal money coming into Freeport, employment opportunities were still limited for communities of color. Locally elected officials distributed hiring and federal aid. A *New York Amsterdam News* editorial stated, "The White workingman has a monopoly on relief projects. Negro families are not given dollar for dollar with Whites for rent and labor."[28] In a local editorial, African American lawyer and new Republican committeeman of Nassau County Moxey Rigby stated, "The Black Community needs jobs, and New Deal is making the community soft."[29]

As New Deal funds diverted from communities of color, the seaside resorts (staples for working-class locals) went out of business. Communities such as Bennington Park suffered. Bennington Park soon became run-down, and the vibrant village was dotted with vacant stores. In the mid-1930s, the Roosevelt administration established the National Youth Administration (NYA), which focused on the employment of sixteen- to twenty-five-year-olds and had a separate division focused on Black unemployment. The agency operated until 1943, but in the late 1930s and early 1940s, Charles Ferguson and his family found temporary employment to relieve some of the economic tensions his family was enduring. Alma was a domestic worker and, later in the 1940 census, was listed as a stay-at-home mother with no reported income and widowed; she depended on the income of her sons for household expenses. This need for income conflicted with her sons' desires to attain high school diplomas.

Charles and Edward received some high school education but never graduated. Alphonso, Richard, and Joseph completed elementary school, and Minnie completed the eighth grade. The lack of education further limited the Ferguson family's opportunities for good-paying jobs. The Fergusons were not the only family of color who faced this dilemma. The Freeport High School graduating class of 1935 (Charles's anticipated

This page: Pictured are Bennington Park homes after years of neglect. Freeport village's budget had deep cuts during the Great Depression, which affected communities of color such as Bennington. *Courtesy of Freeport Historical Society.*

graduating class) had 180 graduates. Of the 180 graduates, 177 were white, and 3 were persons of color (Freeport and Roosevelt shared a high school). The racial disparity between white and Black high school graduates continued well into the next few decades. Charles's older brother Edward became a laborer for the Works Progress Administration, Alphonso became a tree skinner for the NYA, and Joseph and Richard, who were sixteen and fifteen years old, were listed as unemployed in the 1940 census. The laborer positions with the WPA were limited in income and hours. In 1939, Charles was unemployed for forty weeks, worked only twelve weeks, and generated a yearly income of $216. Similarly, Alphonso had an annual income of $216 and was unemployed and employed simultaneously. Edward was the breadwinner of the household. Edward worked thirty-two weeks in 1939, was unemployed for twenty, and brought home an income of $357 that year. The monthly rent of their Bennett Avenue home was $25. Minnie generated no revenue in 1939. Minnie's household, next to the Ferguson family, generated $1,002 per year between the eleven family members and paid $15 per month in rent.

Coming into adulthood, Charles, Alphonso, Richard, Joseph, and Edward faced a combination of limited opportunities and the social effects of poverty. Despite the jobs provided by the WPA, balancing daily expenses and paying rent on time was a constant struggle. Due to these factors, Charles and Alphonso had brief run-ins with the law. Charles was convicted of attempted burglary in the third degree. Alphonso was convicted twice of disorderly conduct and sentenced to fifteen days in jail. With the economic conditions and two of her sons getting caught up in the legal system, Alma started to get into heated arguments with her sons over money. In one of these arguments with Alphonso, Alma stabbed him with a knife in his back and punctured his left lung. Alphonso was hospitalized in critical condition. Alma was arrested that night, and Joseph was held as a material witness to the event. Alma was convicted of first-degree assault on her son and was confined to Albion State Training School, which serviced women with mental health challenges. Alphonso fully recovered from his wound, emotional scars notwithstanding. With these personal family struggles, Charles, Richard, Joseph, and Edward constantly sought opportunities outside their community. One of these opportunities led them into the United States armed service.

Chapter 6

WORLD WAR II MOBILIZATION

Charles, Richard, Joseph, and Edward's Military Service

Before the United States entered World War II, there was a strong national desire to stay neutral or adopt an isolationist global stance. Following the outbreak of war in 1939, most Americans did not want to get involved but supported selling supplies to England. But as the war progressed, public views changed. According to a study on American public opinion and World War II from the political science department of the Massachusetts Institute of Technology, support shifted in 1940, with 67 percent of Americans saying that it should be a priority to help England by any means necessary. The public opinion study reflected that 33 percent of respondents believed it was important for Americans to stay neutral or out of the war altogether. The American First Committee, formed in late 1940, advocated neutrality. A spokesperson for the committee, Charles Lindbergh, stated, "The Jewish people are one of the groups pressing us [United States] for war with Europe." The American First Committee had an estimated membership of 800,000 from more than 400 chapters across every major city in the United States.

The most robust demand for neutrality came from American pro-fascist groups. By the late 1930s, many white supremacist sentiments had evolved into militaristic ideologies. The Christian Front—founded on the racist broadcasts of Charles Coughlin, who advocated for the rise of fascism as the only effective fight against the spread of communism—was gaining in membership. Coughlin based his ideology on the claim that "Jews had started the Russian and Spanish revolutions, in a struggle between

Christian civilization and Jewish backed communism." As America drew closer toward the war, Coughlin demanded his followers arm themselves and prepare for "war against the Jewish Communists in American streets." Following his call to arms, Christian Front, other Coughlin-inspired groups, and Iron Guard, a pro-fascist organization, formed militias under the guise of local sporting or rifle clubs.[30] These militia platoons formed in secret outside New York City. The Christian Front claimed it had a 5-million-man army ready. In January 1940, headlines ran a story of an attempted overthrow of the United States by the Brooklyn chapter of the Christian Front. Chapter leader John F. Cassidy and right-wing militant William Gerald Bishop developed military-style training camps in Sullivan County, recruiting multiple active members of the state national guard. After an extensive FBI investigation, agents concluded that Bishop was a native-born Austrian with questionable connections to Nazi Germany.

The most visible local pro-fascist groups were the German Bunds. The Bund/Nazi nationalist groups gained a New York metro area base. The Bund campaigned to keep America neutral and help American Germans go back to Germany to fight for the fatherland while furthering anti-Semitism. On Long Island, the German Bund built one of its largest fundraising divisions for the American Nazi cause: Camp Siegfried. Tucked away in Yaphank, Suffolk County, thirty miles east of Freeport, Camp Siegfried sold an average of $123,000 in Nazi bonds each summer. Summer camp activities at Siegfried included paramilitary activities and teaching of Nazi ideals. As thousands attended the activities and participated in the fundraisers, Nazi ambassadors recruited Bund members in military aviation engineering to become spies for Hitler's war machine. One person recruited in Yaphank was Erich Traub, a New York resident and graduate of the Rockefeller Institute in virology. After being recruited, Traub moved to Nazi Germany and worked under Heinrich Himmler to develop the Nazis' biological warfare program. (After the war, Traub was brought back to the United States through Operation Paper Clip and became one of the founders of Plum Island animal disease and germ warfare laboratory.) Despite the rise in pro-fascist/militaristic racist groups, communities of color across New York were split on the idea of staying neutral. One argument highlighted by the Black-owned *New York Amsterdam News* was as follows: "Yes, under Hitler, Black people will not fare well, but Hitler is applying the same colonization over the English, which is the same economic and political oppression of the African fostered by the British Empire and France."[31] Other views expressed were in a September 1941 *New York Amsterdam* editorial:

> *The Negro population in the United States tells any story; it is that Christianity, democracy, and hypocrisy travel together as inseparable bedfellows. Fascism can have little if any serious consequences for the Negro here. He has been a victim of the most severe forms of Fascism for 300 years, and even now that we prate about democracy as though we believe in its principles, the Negro still suffers under American Fascism.*[32]

Counterarguments advocated for "all-out aid to Britain, which will convoy a demand for ships but not declare war against Germany."[33] But a growing view within the communities of color was echoed by civil rights leader and writer William Pickens. In speeches throughout Harlem and other New York communities of color, Pickens stated, "The Nazis are 100% of a Menace to the Jews and Negros." Pickens further advocated for the community to buy liberty bonds. (After the United States declared war, these bonds became war bonds.)

With the divided but growing public support and the aggressive expansion of the Axis Powers in Europe and Asia, the United States took proactive steps to build up its military. The Selective Training and Service Act of 1940 enabled the Selective Service System to start mobilization on a local level. All records and personnel files were managed locally. These local boards' responsibility was to oversee the registration of all males over eighteen for service. Most of the estimated one million New Yorkers who served in the military during World War II would have had their first stop at the local draft board. The Hempstead Draft Board became the most active one in Nassau County.[34] By 1940, the Hempstead Board had processed 480 men from January to June 30, 1941. The board set individual quotas for the largest Nassau County towns. Freeport/Roosevelt had thirteen men register in January alone, but all Black draftees were deferred until February or when the Black draft units were organized.[35] Delays of draft boards accepting inductees of color came with some criticism. One editorial in the *Amsterdam News* stated:

> *Full rights to equal participation in national defense are needed. For instance, no Negro is accepted in the Navy except for mess hall roles or denied enlisting in the Marines. Those who want to defend democracy against Hitler's assault from without must also take action to win democracy at home on the inter-racial front. Practicing racial discrimination endangers our defense by undermining the necessary democratic morale, which is playing Hitler's game.*[36]

The discrimination in the armed services got the attention of the NAACP, which launched an investigation in late 1941 to report how people of color were treated in the military and national defense industries. In response to the discrimination in ranks, Admiral Chester W. Nimitz argued that "Negros in the navy could hold higher ranks, which would, in general, could be superior to Whites who enlist as petty officers and the enlisted Whites would not stand for this."[37] But as 1941 drew to a close, all these relics of Jim Crow in the armed services and structures that kept employment discrimination in place would be challenged. The United States was entering a total war. Every part of society would become an active participant in the deadliest conflict in human history.

"December 7, 1941, a date that will live in infamy" was announced on radios across the United States during President Roosevelt's broadcast. The Japanese had bombed the U.S. naval base in Pearl Harbor. The following day, December 8, the United States declared war on Japan, after which all Axis Powers declared war on the United States. Across the country's communities of color, the heroic actions of Doris Miller, a Black mess attendant serving on the battleship *West Virginia* during the Japanese attack on Pearl Harbor, became immortalized. Miller saved several sailors and the captain and operated the antiaircraft machine gun on the deck until all the rounds were exhausted. On May 27, 1942, Miller was awarded the Navy Cross, the service's third-highest honor. The Navy Cross was bestowed on Miller by Admiral Chester Nimitz, who had made headlines a year earlier advocating for a "barring of Negros in the Navy." Miller's actions and recognition became an inspiration for the two and a half million Black men and women who served in the armed forces during World War II.

Before reaching the 2.5-million-person peak, Black soldiers were limited to nine jobs with a 50,000-soldier cap for the army. These roles included artillery, engineering, and 2,250 soldiers for the domestic air corps. This domestic air corps was the foundation of the Tuskegee Airmen. Many other initial jobs for soldiers of color were menial, such as mess hall attendants. But despite these limited roles, the *Amsterdam Star* called for unity among all people of color in editorials. One stated, "In this thrust of a nation [referring to the Japanese attack on Pearl Harbor] of one mind, there are no races or classes or sections: there are no Negroes or Jews or Whites. Now, if ever, we stand together. Americans all—all out for America."[38] While the mobilization of Black units was being pushed, Jim Crow stereotypes persisted in the armed service. Like in World War I, World War II saw racially segregated units. Despite the mobilization in communities of color and the heroic actions

Black soldiers shipping out from New York City into the European theater of war. *Courtesy of New York Public Library.*

of Doris Miller, segregated Black units were not trusted by the military command for combat roles. At the same time, the United Stated increased mobilization efforts, civil rights groups pushed to combat racial stereotypes in the military ranks. From this push came the ending of the 50,000-soldier cap and some of the most legendary units ever established.

The Tuskegee Airmen, the most famous Black unit, was started in June 1941 before America's involvement in the war. The training lasted a total of eight months, in three ten-week sections. The total number of airmen trained was 994. Of this number, 450 would see combat, fly fifteen thousand missions and receive 150 Flying Crosses. These men would be part of the 99th Pursuit Squadron. The first squadron to go overseas was the 332nd Fighter Group, in either a Curtis P-40 or Long Island's flagship plane, the Republic P-47 Thunderbolt.[39] The company also flew in the P-51 Mustang, which was issued later in the war. The biggest claim to fame of the Tuskegee Airmen was that it never lost a single bomber to enemy fighters in two hundred escort missions over Europe.[40] The airmen later in the war would serve for the 477th Bombardment Group. The Tuskegee Airmen became heroes, with their actions on the headlines of every major newspaper, which later referred to them as "Red Tails" (referring to the color of the tail wing on the P-51 Mustangs). Local Tuskegee Airman Charles Dryden recalled in an interview, "I was excited by the prospect of being the first to shoot down a Nazi plane in my pack. This excitement came from the desire for recognition and a strong desire to show that the Nazi ideology of a supreme Aryan race was false. The best way to prove that was to have a Black person shoot down a Nazi plane."[41] Dryden's first time downing a Nazi aircraft was part of a series of raids against the Italian island of Pantelleria, which the airmen would call the "panty raids." After a series of air-to-ground bombardments, the Nazis surrendered the island. This victory led the airmen to upgrade to the desirable P-51 Mustang for air-to-ground raids. Despite wins in the battle for Pantelleria, Dryden and the other airmen did not receive respect from their white counterparts. Tuskegee men were not allowed to attend the same clubs on base, and back in the States, German POWs were permitted to eat in the same mess hall as whites, while Black soldiers were confined to a separate section. Worst of all, white soldiers of lower ranks often would not salute higher-ranked Black soldiers. Fellow airman and Glen Cove native William "Joe" Johnson was shocked at the racism he witnessed while training in the South and during deployment among fellow white soldiers: "They talked about racism and whatnot in Germany in Europe, the Nazis. Here, it was bad with lynching and was not discussed as a problem among the soldiers."[42]

The second deployment of men from Tuskegee training included Amityville native Samuel Leftenant. The Leftenant family came to Amityville from Goose Creek, South Carolina, during the Great Depression. The family hoped to find more economic opportunities and lived in a two-room house in living conditions similar to what they had known back in Goose Creek. The family became well known within the Bethel AME Church on Albany Avenue, which earned them respect within the community. Samuel, looking for additional opportunities, enlisted and was stationed at the Ramitelli air base in Italy. On April 12, 1945, over Austria, Leftenant was flying his third mission in his P-51 Mustang alongside flight leader James Hall; they were escorting American bombers en route to Germany. Halfway through the mission, Leftenant's and Hall's planes collided in the air, and both airmen jumped out. Leftenant was never seen again, and Nazis captured Hall. First, Leftenant was declared Missing in Action (MIA), but later, in 1946, he was reclassified as a Killed

Tuskegee Airmen in training exiting the parachute room. *Courtesy of the National Achieves.*

in Action (KIA). Samuel became immortalized as a hometown hero, and his service inspired others within his community to enlist, including his sister Nancy, who signed up with the Army Nurse Cadets.

Other units of color with strong enlistment bases on Long Island and New York City were the 92nd and 93rd Infantry Divisions, known as the Buffalo Division. The 92nd and 93rd divisions had their roots in the conquest of the American frontier. Soldiers from these divisions, originally established after the Civil War, were formerly enslaved men who had signed up for opportunities to escape Black Americans' post–Civil War persecution. Less than a century later, many Black Americans viewed these armed service divisions as a haven from structural racism in the North and South. Aquebogue native Thomas Watkins, the son of a farmworker, suffered discrimination at Riverhead High School. His teachers pushed him away from the idea of going to college and encouraged him to accept a job as a groundskeeper. While working as a caddy for the Shinnecock Hills Country Club in South Hampton, Watkins desperately sought new opportunities. Like the generations of Buffalo Soldiers before him, Watkins signed up for the service to escape bigotry, racism, and limited employment opportunities. Following his enlistment, Watkins befriended Huntington native Earl Johnson, who had signed up for the army after the bombing of Pearl Harbor. Although they were enlisted, the men did not see combat until the war department lifted the ban on Black soldiers serving in the infantry. Watkins and Johnson were the first soldiers of the Buffalo Divisions to see the battle. Both men fought along the Arno River in Italy in 1944 and witnessed the legendary actions of John Fox, who saw himself getting overrun by Germans and called an airstrike on himself to take out the German troops. His unit sustained heavy casualties, but it played a crucial role in defeating the Axis forces in Italy. Back home in the United States,

On Easter morning, William E. Thomas and Private First Class Joseph Black holding up artillery shells reading "Happy Easter Adolph." *Courtesy of National Archives.*

these soldiers' bravery was in the headlines of many newspapers, which further worked as an inspiration for people of color to enlist.

Charles Ferguson's enlistment picture into the Army Air Corps, 1941. *Courtesy of Wilfred Ferguson.*

Before the courage of the Tuskegee Airmen and the 92nd and 93rd Buffalo Soldier Divisions, the two elder Ferguson brothers enlisted. The first was Charles, who enlisted in the U.S. Army Air Corps (later referred to as the Army Air Force) on February 6, 1941. Charles and Edward most likely enlisted to secure more opportunities for their families due to their employment limitations in pre–World War II Nassau County. Before Charles enlisted, he married his eighteen-year-old neighbor Minnie Jackson on February 21, 1940. Soon after their marriage, their first son, Charles Ferguson Jr., was born on April 4, 1940. His second son, Richard, was born on February 22, 1942, and his third, Wilfred, was born in 1943. By the close of his overseas service, Charles had been promoted to the rank of private first class. Edward enlisted in the army in May 1941 and was sent to Camp Upton, Yaphank, New York, for basic training. After training, he was stationed with an infantry unit at Fort Sill, Oklahoma.[43] By June 1943, Edward had earned a promotion in rank to corporal.

Following his elder brothers' footsteps, Richard enlisted in the army on August 30, 1943, as a private. Following basic training, he was shipped out to Europe and fought with the Third Army in Germany under the command of General George Patton. Due to a fire at the National Archives in the 1970s, most of Richard's records were lost, and his exact unit cannot be confirmed. During Richard's service, one of the most famous Black units of the Third Army in Germany was the 761st Tank Battalion, the Black Panthers. After the battalion came to shore at Omaha Beach, Patton gave one of his most famous speeches: "Men, you are the first Negro tankers to ever fight in the American Army. I would never have asked for you if you weren't good. I have nothing but the best in my army. Everyone has their eyes on you. Most of all, your race is looking forward to your success. Don't let them down, and damn you, don't let me down."

Black air corps paratroopers training at Craig Field, Selma, Alabama. This is where Charles Ferguson trained as a paratrooper. *Courtesy of National Archives.*

Joseph enlisted in the navy on June 25, 1943, at sixteen. He was stationed at various local bases stateside before being shipped to the Pacific Theater. Alphonso was the only brother not to serve in the armed services. According to Alphonso's draft card, his height was five feet, two inches; his weight was 116 pounds, and he might have been suffering from health problems. During the war, Alphonso got a job at the Texas Ranger restaurant in Freeport.

The military service of the four brothers came with reminders of Jim Crow racial boundaries, especially Charles's time in Fort Benning. Like many people of color, Charles Felix Hall enlisted a year before seeking more opportunities. Charles was sent to Fort Benning, Georgia, for basic training in late February 1941. While Charles Ferguson was at Fort Benning, Private Hall went missing after being seen near an all-white part of town surrounding the base. Days earlier, Hall had refused to address a white local as "Sir," resulting in an argument.[44] In the month that followed, after a routine training exercise, soldiers found Hall's decomposing body in the woods with a noose around his neck and his feet bound. His murder would haunt the soldiers of the Black units training at Fort Benning and reminded them of the contradictions of being shipped off to Europe to fight tyranny while bearing witness to enforced and often unwritten Jim Crow laws.

Like other soldiers of color, the Fergusons were in racially segregated units. Only at the close of the war did generals strongly opposed to Black soldiers fighting in active combat, such as Dwight Eisenhower in the European Theater, shift their views on race. Following the successes of Black fighter squadrons, like the 92nd and 93rd Buffalo Divisions, 761st Tank Battalion, and the Tuskegee Airmen, General Eisenhower became vocal in commending the grit and courage of Black soldiers in combat. In the Pacific Theater, General Douglas MacArthur, who had never opposed the use of Black soldiers, shared the sentiment of Eisenhower that Black soldiers' courage and determination had distinguished them on the battlefield.[45] The brave actions of these soldiers helped prove racist ideology wrong, and the military shifted its view of segregated units as liabilities.[46] At the advice of all the generals at the close of the war, President Harry Truman issued Executive Order 9981, integrating every branch of the service.

Chapter 7

WAR PRODUCTION AND THE DOMESTIC FIGHT FOR CIVIL RIGHTS

The debate over whether communities of color would support the war was settled. The influx of Black enlistees into the armed services and their actions on the battlefield gave the United States an advantage over the Axis Powers. But World War II was a total war, meaning it would require all American society to win the war. Building an industrial wartime economy from a society still in the grips of the Great Depression and largely underdeveloped would require all hands on deck. This economic shift would require communities of color to be integrated into the wartime effort. In turn, it would bring potential new economic opportunities for communities of color and legal protections against discrimination to ensure their participation.

Long Island, a rural appendage of New York City, had an aviation manufacturing economy installed from the 1920s but was underdeveloped. The most significant potential for industrial development in the counties of Nassau and Suffolk had been the connection of railroad lines to New York City harbors and the system of parkways built in the decade prior. Most needed was a robust workforce trained in aviation manufacturing. In creating a war-based economy, nothing can be overlooked, and old ingrained biases must be confronted. The non-white communities across Long Island, kept isolated by centuries of socially constructed racial boundaries, would have to be upended to free up a labor force. New York City communities of color did not see economic opportunity in Long Island following the decline of South Shore resort communities, but that changed as the economy shifted to manufacturing. This increased demand for labor became an opportunity for civil rights protections. Discrimination in hiring was an economic issue that set limits on an expanding labor force. Encapsulating the Black community's sentiment was an editorial in the *Pittsburgh Courier*, written by Black factory worker James Thompson, who pondered, "Should I Sacrifice to Live Half American? The V displayed across America represents a victory against Axis Powers' tyranny, slavery, and aggression. We need a double VV for the victory sign. The first V stood for the victory of enemies and a second V for victory over enemies from within the United States that limit freedoms of the African American."[47] On February 14, the *Courier*'s staff editor responded and further cemented Thompson's editorial by stating:

> *We, as colored Americans, are determined to protect our country, our form of government, and the freedoms we cherish for ourselves and the rest of the world; therefore, we have adopted the Double "V" war cry—victory over our enemies on the battlefields abroad. Thus in our fight for freedom, we wage a two-pronged attack against our enslavers at home and those abroad who would enslave us. We Have a Stake in this Fight.... We Are Americans Too!*[48]

The *Courier* was one of the most prominent Black newspapers in the country, with a daily circulation of more than 200,000 throughout all-Black communities. Weeks prior, the paper ran a campaign against the American

Participants in the "Double V" campaign mobilizing volunteers for civilian defense. *Courtesy of National Archives.*

The "Double V" campaign encouraged volunteers for the war effort and promoted the sales of war bonds. The U.S. Office of Treasury commissioned bond posters for the Black community. *Courtesy of the National African American History and Culture Museum.*

Right: New Yorker Charity Adams of the Women's Army Auxiliary Corps recruiting volunteers. *Courtesy of New York Public Library.*

Below: The June 1942 "Double V" rally in New York was held at Madison Square Garden. This rally was the largest Double V rally, named the "Great Pageant of Hope." *Courtesy of New York Public Library.*

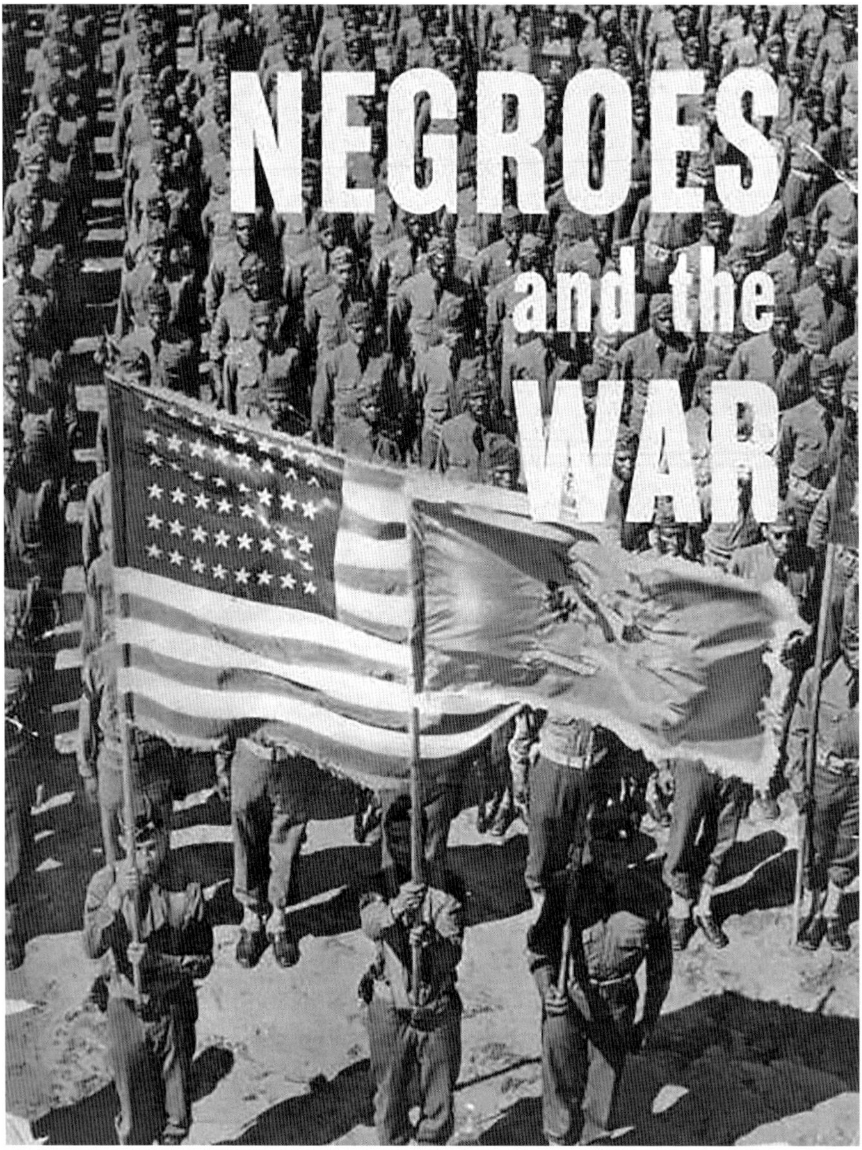

Above: The cover of the program bulletin from the "Great Pageant of Hope." The cover image shows 41st Engineers at Fort Bragg, North Carolina, in color guard ceremony. *Courtesy of New York Public Library.*

Opposite: Another circulated program bulletin from the Madison Square Garden rally. The bulletin details the connection between Hitlerism ideals and Jim Crow. *Courtesy of New York Public Library.*

Red Cross for its refusal to accept Black blood donors. Combined with the Thompson editorial and the Red Cross campaign, a patriotic rallying call to demand the Black community to contribute with no limitations to the war effort was in lockstep with civil rights fights. Soon followed were local Double V clubs, which organized victory bond drives. In June 1942, the biggest Double V rally in New York was at Madison Square Garden. The rally advertised itself as the "Great Pageant of Hope," with an agenda that discussed ways to defeat Hitler, Jim Crow, and anti-Semitism. After the rally, Double V ideals gained more traction with an editorial by Oswald Villard, featured in *Newsday* and the *New York Evening Post*. Villard, a noted journalist, editor of the *Evening Post* and one of the founders of the NAACP, stated:

> *When men have cause and can stand up and demand their rights without compromise, they are certain to succeed in the long term. Here the Negro is backing the government's war effort and demanding that it shall cease being a hypocrite, cease having two classes of citizens, and cease giving ammunition to the Axis powers by continuing to deprive Colored Americans of their constitutional rights in both war and peace.*[49]

Following the Double V clubs' establishment and the Madison Square Garden's "Great Pageant of Hope," government officials grew concerned that the campaign could evolve into people of color not supporting the war effort when support was most needed.[50] As government officials grew concerned, celebrities active in the war effort weaved the Double V campaign into patriotism. Actress Lana Turner, who broke war bond sales records by stating that she would kiss any man who purchased $50,000 worth of bonds, frequently gave the Double V campaign symbol to reflect solidarity. In a political endorsement of the campaign, presidential candidate Wendell Willkie wore a Double V pin on his suit lapel.[51] By 1942, the campaign had merged into the national victory campaign focusing solely on an American victory over tyranny. The most significant effect of this campaign was that it pushed for the implementation of Franklin Roosevelt's Executive Order 8802, which banned racial discrimination in U.S. defense industries or companies fulfilling governmental defense contracts. On June 25, 1941, the initial order had very little power for enforcement, but New York built on this executive order to effect its first statewide law against workplace discrimination.

Before the United States declared war, demand for military goods set production records, affecting the once sluggish growth of the aviation manufacturing sector across Long Island. Republic Aviation, in March 1940, introduced the P-43 Lancer and had orders coming in from China for a few hundred planes. In 1937, Grumman tested the F4F Wildcat, which, once introduced in December 1940, came with orders from the United States military, the British Royal Navy, and the Royal Canadian Navy. Orders for the new Wildcat totaled more than seven thousand planes. Grumman's ability to outproduce and outsell its rival Republic created a sense of urgency for Republic. In response, Republic expanded a trade program to educate eight thousand men annually who would become aviation mechanic apprentices upon graduation. Of the initial few thousand students, all were white. The other realization Republic discovered was that it came nowhere near the eight-thousand-man goal.

Long Island's other biggest manufacturers—Brewster Aviation, Grumman Aircraft, and Sperry Gyroscope Corporation—reported a massive labor shortage due to military orders from Europe, Asia, and the United States. Employment discrimination that kept groups out of labor pools was considered a liability for policymakers and aviation executives. An editorial in the *Amsterdam News* noted, "Racial prejudices are so strongly embedded in our industrial fabric that a Black man's patriotism is no recommendation. These are thousands of Negroes who can offer skill and patriotism. Not suppressing anti-racial feelings in a time of an approaching world emergency is an act of industrial sabotage itself."[52]

To free the labor pool, Governor Herbert Lehman created the temporary Discrimination in Employment Committee in early 1941. In a speech outlining the committee, Lehman stated, "At a time when the need for extending industrial activity is calling forth the utmost effort of both public and private organizations, it is unpardonable for us not to find a way to use the labor resources which minority groups represent."[53] This committee examined all cases of labor discrimination from defense contractors. Building on the discrimination law, New York added three amendments, including making it illegal to refuse employment and union membership because of race, creed, and color and using applications to inquire about applicants' race or creed.[54] To strengthen the state discrimination committee, the governor created a compliance board. This new board replaced an initially proposed inquiry committee. The new committee focused on defense plant jobs, defense manufacturing-based unions, and defense training schools. The newly organized committee appointed Chairperson Frieda Miller, who organized investigations into hiring practices that prevented people from getting hired based on race, color, and national origin. Before the new committee, only 4 percent of Black citizens were in defense vocational schools throughout the state. Lieutenant Governor Charles Poletti stated that the vocational programs should have at least 8 percent.[55] Roosevelt's executive order and state committees, such as New York State's Discrimination Committee, created one of the most significant employment gains for Black women, particularly in industrial occupations. These gains reflected a rise from 6.5 percent to 18 percent employment and an overall 40 percent wage increase for all labor demographics across defense industry positions.[56]

On April 8, 1943, the state discrimination board faced one of its many tests in Nassau County. Black men and women were completing aviation programs but were not getting hired.[57] Several people filed a discrimination complaint, stating that "after they completed courses in defense schools, they had been given a runaround by war plants, or refused to hire them without explanation." Following this and other complaints across the county, most Long Island defense plants came under routine monitoring for their hiring practices. One defense plant (not named) had 533 employees but only employed 8 Black people. State monitoring and legislation paved the way for Grumman to hire more than 800 Black men and women, making up more than 3 percent of the Grumman Bethpage workforce. The growth to more than 3 percent became a milestone for the committee because it reflected the demographic of Nassau County, whose citizens of color made up 3 percent of the population.[58]

This page: Black workers at a Republic Aviation plant constructing a P-47 Thunderbolt. *Courtesy of the Library of Congress.*

While monitoring local plants, the committee also reviewed complaints of Jewish people being dismissed on security concerns, leading lawmakers to extend the discrimination regulations to include religious groups. The council freed up some of the labor pool needed, but when the United States declared war, the labor pool was at risk of being drafted. Two deferments were added to the draft within the Selective Service Act. Deferment 11-B was based on wartime production, and 11-B (H) was based on wartime production but covered ages thirty-eight to forty-four. These deferments were granted locally and, in many cases, were used to prevent workers from unionizing in smaller plants. Freeport's Columbian Bronze Corporation was contracted to make propellers for the navy. The working conditions at Columbian were hazardous. Workers suffered from sore throats and other breathing problems because they were not provided with protective wear from heavy dust and airborne fibers. There were also no water fountains or proper bathrooms. In response, workers started walking off the job and striking. The company's reaction was to notify Freeport Selective Service Board to have striking workers reclassified as class I-A. This reclassification made them eligible to be drafted into military service. After examining all the Nassau County draft boards, Freeport's was the only board drafting men over age twenty-six who had previously been classified as essential wartime workers. The reclassification of the striking workers prompted an investigation by New York selective service director Ames T. Brown. His investigation concluded that Freeport's numbers were due to a misinterpretation of the guidelines of factory managers and draft board workers.[59] Columbian Bronze Corporation's success in getting striking workers drafted and similar actions from other plants might have limited all workforce complaints from fear of retribution in local industries. Wage and workplace discrimination complaints to New York State's Discrimination Committee may also have been influenced by war manufacturing companies' influence on local draft boards.

Once elected governor, Thomas Dewey started to work on a civil rights law to cement the gains of the Lehman administration. This law would be the first of its kind in the country. By March 12, 1945, the New York legislature had passed the Ives-Quinn Act (the New York State Civil Rights Law). The law's purpose was to eliminate and prevent discrimination based on race, creed, color, or national origin by employers, labor organizations, employment agencies, or other persons.[60] The law made the temporary employment discrimination boards established by former governor Lehman permanent, with five commissioners appointed to five-year terms. Commissioners' powers were extended, including the authority to formulate policies for the state in combating discrimination and investigating claims of discrimination and retaliation against the complainant. In a *Newsday* editorial about the law, the editor stated, "Discrimination usually comes about because of deep-seated irrational prejudice on the part of the discriminator. People don't reform their emotions or attitudes just because somebody passes a law. Long Island itself is not free of this ugly prejudice. Suffolk is fighting white against Black, Nassau, and Suffolk; some employers bar Catholics because of their religion. The law can help, but real tolerance must come from within ourselves."[61] On June 29, Henry Turner, the first commissioner under the new civil rights law, was appointed. In a statement, Turner said, "There shall be no discrimination on the grounds of race, creed, color or national origin—that every citizen of our state has a right to earn his bread through gainful employment without discrimination or prejudice."[62] Many questions about the law were left unanswered following the Turner press conference. Did the law apply to the segregation of public and private facilities? What were the penalties for violating the law?

Long Island had no laws that enforced segregation of public facilities, but some restaurants and other businesses practiced racial segregation in their establishments. Common practices in some movie theaters included racially separated sections, enforced by an usher guiding you to a specific seat, and some restaurants refused to serve Black patrons. The passage of the civil rights law offered a potential end to these practices. On July 22, 1945, the law had its first test. Blandena Lee, her daughter, and a friend, Black residents of Franklin Square, entered Franklin Square Grill on Hempstead Turnpike. This was the first time they visited the diner minutes from their residence. But once they entered the establishment, a waitress ushered them to the grill counter section of the restaurant. Lee, in response, requested a booth in a nearly empty section. The waitress told them that all the seats in the dining area were reserved. Lee then asked manager Albert Downward if all the seats were reserved. Downward replied, "Yes, they are all reserved." Despite this, Lee and the two others sat at a table and said, "We will gladly move when the reserved party comes." The waitress replied, "You can sit there all night, and you won't be served."[63] While waiting to be served, no one came, and their table was stripped. White patrons came in, sat down, and were served as they waited.

After fifty minutes, Lee, her daughter, and her friend left. Following the event, Lee contacted the Hempstead Branch of the NAACP. After she reported the incident to branch president Alberta Gray, she contacted national NAACP headquarters in New York City, and a complaint was petitioned in Hempstead District Court. The district attorney filed charges against Albert Downward for violating the newly passed New York State Civil Rights Law. Downward pleaded not guilty and claimed that the table was reserved and that he had offered an alternative seating arrangement. The trial date was set to start on February 1, 1946. Communities of color across Long Island took notice of the court case—a guilty verdict would validate that progress was being made. The verdict arrived on February 5 after forty-five minutes of deliberation. But the not-guilty verdict for Downward was overshadowed by a cataclysmic event in the early morning hours of February 5 in Freeport, soon to headline newspapers across the country.

Chapter 8

FEBRUARY 5, 1946

The eyewitness accounts from the early, predawn hours of February 5 vary. The events of that morning remain ingrained as generational trauma for the Ferguson family. In the community of Freeport, these events reflected covert and overt racial biases that had been simmering for more than a century. For the United States, these events represented the lack of civil rights progress in a swiftly changing society. Postwar racial violence and racially motivated arrests/trials would become the center of newspaper headlines throughout the country. One of the most notorious acts of such violence was the beating and blinding of Black army sergeant Isaac Woodard. In early February 1946, Woodard caught a bus from South Carolina to New York City in his uniform. He had recently received his honorable discharge and had returned home from the Pacific Theater. While waiting for a scheduled departure at a bus stop, Woodard asked the bus driver if he could use the bathroom at a pharmacy. The white bus driver yelled at Woodard and called him various racial slurs in response to his request. The bus driver's remarks started an argument, leading to two white police officers taking Woodard off the bus. Woodard did not resist as the cops removed him from the bus, but the officer started beating him and then gouged out his eyes with their nightsticks, blinding him.[64] The blinding of Woodard became a catalyst for the postwar civil rights movement, but this event happened on February 12, 1946. Most historians debate the first postwar racial violence against Black soldiers did not start with Woodard but rather with the events in Freeport on February 5, 1946.

On February 4, 1946, Charles Ferguson had plans to celebrate his reenlistment into a Black paratrooper unit (Charles's unit could not be confirmed, but it was believed to be the 555th Parachute Infantry Battalion) in his hometown. Before reenlistment, Charles had served overseas and received a promotion to private first class. While stationed at Craig Field, Selma, Alabama Air Corps Base, Charles reenlisted on December 22, 1945. He was sent to Greensboro, North Carolina, for paratrooper training, but he was granted a leave in early February and promptly went home to see his family. On the afternoon of February 4, Charles, dressed in his military uniform, kissed his wife, Minnie, and said goodbye to his three sons, Charles, Wilfred, and Richard. Leaving his home at 60 Francis Street, Roosevelt, he met up with his brothers Richard, Joseph, and Alphonso. The brothers then met at their childhood home at 93 Bennett Avenue in Roosevelt. While serving as a navy cook, Joseph was stationed on a boat docked in Lido Beach following five months in the Pacific. On leave, Joseph planned to unite with his brothers in full military uniform. Joseph was the last to arrive at the Bennett Avenue residence. Richard got dressed in his military attire at the Bennett Avenue home. Richard was discharged in November following a truck accident in Europe in which he was injured. Upon his discharge, he held the rank of private in the army and received monthly separation payments. While Alphonso was getting ready in the other room of their home, Charles arrived and, later, Joseph. Since their father died, Alphonso and Richard had been paying for the upkeep and monthly expenses at the Bennett Avenue home.

After their various military tours of duty, the four united for the first time in three years. Once together, four of the five brothers shared stories and embraced. While deciding what to do that night, Richard strummed on a guitar and sang as Charles, Joseph, and Allie (the brothers' nickname for Alphonso) argued whether to go to New York City or stay local. They agreed to make New York City part of the plans, but first, they wanted to get pictures done in Hempstead displaying their ranks and military achievements. They all left the house between 6:00 p.m. and 9:00 p.m. for Hempstead. While in Hempstead, the four brothers reminisced with neighborhood stories and shared events they encountered while in the service over multiple beers at a Hempstead beer garden named Eddie's. After passing the time at the beer garden, they walked a few blocks to another beer garden and drank three more beers. Richard broke the trend and ordered three to four glasses of wine at the second location. After this visit, the brothers boarded a bus for Freeport to get a late-night snack at the Texas Ranger. While on the bus, Madeline

Moher and her fifteen-year-old daughter Joan Vollmer were returning from the Winter Carnival in Mineola. The brothers got on the bus and rode with them for twenty minutes before arriving in Freeport. Moher witnessed the brothers "standing in the crowded bus, having a good time, but polite and did not appear disorderly."[65] Arriving at Freeport after midnight, they walked over to the Texas Ranger on North Main Street next to the Freeport Motel (the FBI report states that the brothers ate first and then went to get coffee, but the state probe differs). The brothers had the Texas Ranger special (hamburgers with locally famous coleslaw) and coffee but no alcoholic beverages. They stayed at the Texas Ranger for twenty to twenty-five minutes. Charles suggested they go to the coffee shop Freeport Bus Terminal Tea Room behind the Texas Ranger, located on Henry Street, after the meal. Constantin "Gus" Cholakis managed the coffee shop.

At the bus terminal around 12:38 a.m., Madeline Moher and Joan were having coffee and hot chocolate, waiting for the 12:40 a.m. bus to bring them home to Baldwin Harbor. Madeline, in interviews, stated that "the brothers were in good conduct before entering the shop, but when

The Texas Ranger was a short distance from the bus terminal and near the Long Island Rail Road Freeport station. The spot was where the Ferguson brothers stopped and ate before going to the Terminal Tea Room. *Courtesy of Freeport Historical Society.*

they asked for coffee which had a sufficient amount left in the urn, the manager refused to serve them by saying he was out of coffee. But while denying service to the brothers, the manager served the white patrons coffee."[66] Alexander Coleman, a local aviation mechanic, told the press weeks after the incident that he "was not surprised the trouble developed in the Bus Station Tea Room. He recited an earlier incident of entering the tea room with a person of color who was likewise refused service."[67] Moher elaborated further that the brothers did not curse or threaten anyone while she was in the tea room. Moher's story was collaborated by Joe Langdon, who was in the tea room and was the driver for the 12:40 a.m. bus for which Moher and her daughter were waiting. But according to Cholakis, his encounter with the Ferguson brothers differed. The manager stated, "They asked for coffee, but I told them there was no more coffee. One of the brothers then asked for tea or cocoa instead. In response to being denied coffee, Charles called [me] a Greek son of a bitch and attempted to climb across the counter and assault the staff. Two brothers pulled Charles out of the shop outside to calm down."[68] Following the event at the tea room, the brothers went to The Nest, a popular and rowdy club in Bennington Park that was a ten-minute walk. On the way to The Nest, Charles was suspected of breaking a Sinclair and Raynor Oil and Coal Supply office window at 12 Henry Street across from the Terminal Tea Room. Allegedly, Charles had punched or kicked the window as he passed through Henry Street. When the brothers entered The Nest, they told Pernell White, the bartender, that they all

The Terminal Tea Room was centered on the Freeport bus terminal. This is the coffee shop where Charles got into an argument with manager Gus Cholakis. *Courtesy of Freeport Historical Society*).

Pictured is the Sinclair and Raynor Oil and Coal company. This is the building where Charles was suspected of breaking a window after leaving the Terminal Tea Room. *Courtesy of Freeport Historical Society.*

had to use the restroom. While waiting for the restroom, the brothers argued and pushed each other. After using the restroom, they asked for drinks. Pernell then told them no—that they had enough. Charles started to make fun of White's graying hair, and Richard interrupted his brother's insults and stated, "Do not talk to him like that; he is an old man." In later interviews, White noted that the Ferguson brothers left at 1:20 a.m., and he finally closed up at 1:30 a.m.

On foot, Freeport patrol officer Joseph Romeika, Shield No. 22, was making his rounds at the bus terminal. Romeika's assigned shift was from midnight to 8:00 a.m. Romeika was a twenty-six-year-old probationary officer hired about a year and a half before, on June 16, 1945. Before being employed by the Village of Freeport, Romeika was a police officer for the Pennsylvania Railroad and employed by the Burn National Detective Agency. While on probation as a newly hired officer with Freeport, he lived with his sister and brother-in-law on Coram Place within the village of Freeport. Before leaving the station for his shift, Freeport officers debriefed about Nassau County police officer Jack West killed the day before, eight miles away in Mineola. The officers were concerned that his killer was still on the loose. While making his routine check-in with headquarters at a police officer call box next to the tea room, Cholakis called Romeika over. Cholakis told him that the four brothers "threatened his life [in the initial report, it stated that Gus reported he was threatened with a .45-caliber revolver. Cholakis never said he saw the gun but was threatened verbally], and while they were exiting his shop, they broke the window of the office across the street." While surveying the damage, Romeika witnessed the four Ferguson brothers walking back toward the bus terminal. Around the same time, another Black man, Herman Crummell, was walking back from work at Texas Ranger. Herman stayed longer than usual because he was helping his father, also employed at the Ranger, to close up for the night.

Through initial eyewitness accounts, grand jury testimonies, and state investigation, the same chain of events as the brothers lined up against the wall would change in the coming months. The verbal arguments and the escalation differed from eyewitnesses' accounts and police accounts.

Around 1:30 a.m., Romeika, the only officer at the scene, stopped the four brothers, who seemed to be noisy, boisterous, and walking toward the bus terminal. The brothers were walking to catch a bus home. After being stopped, Charles cursed and called Romeika a "son of bitch." Romeika called Charles and his brothers bastards in response and said, "You cannot threaten people." While words were exchanged, the brothers were separated by about twenty-five feet in all—Charles and Richard were close to the officer, with Charles arguing with Romeika, while Joseph and Alphonso were still about twenty-five feet away. Coming around the corner of Henry Street, Crummell recognized the brothers and was called over. (Crummell could not remember which brother called him over.) While exchanging words, Romeika kicked Charles in the groin. Joseph, who moved closer to the altercation, was kicked in the hip by the officer. After the assault on Charles and Joseph, Romeika pulled his service revolver out and ordered the four brothers and Crummell to line up against the Sinclair and Raynor building wall with their hands up. Romeika then went to a nearby telephone pole with a police box to contact headquarters for backup. While the five were against the wall with their hands up, Charles cursed Romeika, calling him names. Romeika, in later statements, recalled Charles telling him, "No white officer was going to arrest me." In contrast to Romeika, the brothers recalled Charles telling the officer, "You get home on leave, and the cops want to lock you up." The officer then claimed Charles shouted, "I may have a .45." Richard, closest to Charles, disputed these accounts. Richard said he had never heard his brother mention a gun or a .45. Charles had lowered his right hand (some accounts said that Charles was falling forward, and some speculated that he was reaching for a handkerchief in his pocket). Romeika, with his service revolver still in hand, fired, hitting Charles in his chest, killing him before he fell to the ground. Within seconds, Romeika also shot Joseph Ferguson through the right shoulder, penetrating the forehead of Alphonso, who was standing behind Joseph. Romeika would later report to his commanding officer that Alphonso lunged toward him, trying to grab his gun, and in response, he shot him.

Following the shootings, Officer Arthur Wulff, who was on patrol three blocks away, arrived with a patrol wagon; Wulff found Romeika with his gun out, standing ten feet in front of the bodies of Charles and Alphonso on the apron of the coal company. After observing the scene, Wulff briefly went to the closest police box and called the police headquarters to request an ambulance. Once the ambulance arrived with a doctor, he pronounced Charles dead; Alphonso was taken to Meadowbrook Hospital and was declared dead seven hours later. Joseph was taken into custody with Richard and Crummell without medical attention. Chief of Police Peter Elar arrived as the wagon loaded up with the prisoners and the ambulance departed. As other officers arrived on the scene, no .45 or any gun was recovered from the brothers—Charles and his brothers were unarmed. Additional officers arriving came in riot gear with tear gas bombs on standby. There was no known threat of civil unrest within the community, and most residents were asleep or unaware of the events at this point in the day. By 4:00 a.m., the entire scene had cleared up. Romeika emptied his .38 Special Smith & Wesson revolver at the precinct in front of Peter Elar. From the six bullets in the chambers, two were shells. Elar instructed Romeika to empty the two shells into his pocket and reload the two missing rounds.

Freeport Police Chief Peter Elar, to whom Romeika had to report following the shooting. *Courtesy of Freeport Historical Society.*

Statements were taken from Gus Cholakis, George Couloras, Herman Crummell, Joseph and Richard Ferguson, and Joseph Romeika. The statements were later recorded in FBI memoranda related to the shooting. These statements were alternately written in either the first or third person. The statements from Joseph and Richard Ferguson, Romeika, and Crummell were taken in the early morning of the shooting by Freeport Police Department officers, Nassau County Police Department officers, and local district attorney Frank Gulotta at the Freeport Police Department.

Gus Cholakis was questioned by Assistant District Attorney Frank Gulotta at the Freeport Police Department at 2:32 a.m., ending at 2:54 am. Witnesses to Cholakis's statement were Captain Stuyvesant Pinnell of Nassau County Police and Sergeant Henry Koekl, and Nathan Birchall recorded it.

Cholakis stated:

> *Around 12:38 am, four negros entered the restaurant and asked for coffee, but we were closing and had no more coffee. I offered the brothers tea or cocoa and remembered seeing them in the restaurant but did not know their names. Only one other person was in the restaurant, George Couloras, who usually reads his newspaper at the counter until closing. After I told the brothers we had no coffee, one of them* [later identified as Charles Ferguson] *began cursing and threatening to kill me. The one threatening me tried to get behind the counter multiple times to strike me but was restrained by his brothers. This bickering continued for about a half-hour until the brothers left and argued outside. I then turned the lights out to discourage them from coming back into the restaurant, which they tried entering again.*

Cholakis continued:

> *As the brothers walked away, I heard one of them break a window of a nearby building over by Sunrise Highway but did not see them break it. I saw the police officer* [later identified as Officer Romeika] *approaching the alley toward the call box on Henry Street. I told the officer that four colored guys tried to murder me, and they went down this way. I could not call the police initially because I could not leave the counter. The officer then called headquarters. After the call, I observed the officer talking to the four people of color adjacent to the terminal. At this distance, I could not see the faces of the four men or hear what they were arguing about, but the officer was facing the men. I then heard two shots and called the police. Later I identified the dead man as the negro that threatened me* [Charles]. *One of the negros I have argued with prior. He came into the restaurant, demanded sandwiches, coffee, and everything, refused to pay, and threatened to kill me. During this occasion, he reached into his back pocket, which made me extremely frightened.*[69]

When asked by Captain Pinnell about Charles's threat, Cholakis stated, "Charles did not threaten [me] with a gun nor a knife the night of the shooting but instead was trying to get at him with his hands and throw things at [me]."

George Couloras was questioned by Assistant District Attorney Frank Gulotta at the Freeport Police Department at 2:55 a.m., ending at 3:01 a.m. Witnesses to Couloras's statement were Captain Stuyvesant Pinnell of Nassau County Police and Sergeant Henry Koekl, and Nathan Birchall recorded it.

George stated:

> *The restaurant was crowded when the argument started, but after the 12:40 a.m. bus departed, the restaurant emptied. Around 12:40 am, the only people in the restaurant were the four negro brothers, Gus and me. I heard a considerable obscene profanity and noticed one of the four negros starting to go behind the counter to hit Gus. I did not do anything out of fear of being hit in the head with a sugar bowl. The brothers then pulled the brother, trying to hit Gus away and out of the restaurant. Gus then called the police and told the officer* [Romeika] *of his trouble with the four negros.*[70]*…I later saw the officer argue with the negros near the coal office by the bus terminal. And then I heard two shots. At this point, I did not leave the restaurant.*

Assistant District Attorney Frank Gulotta questioned Herman Crummell at 3:24 a.m. The cross-examination was witnessed by Captain Stuyvesant Pinnell of the Nassau County Police Department, Sergeant Henry Koehl, Lieutenant Marcel Chagnon, and Chief Elar of the Freeport Police Department and recorded by stenographer Nathan Birchall.

Crummell stated:

> *I was walking back from Sunrise Highway to the Park Inn to get a drink and was walking through the bus terminal area when I saw several negro boys and the police officer arguing.* [Crummell was then standing seven feet from Charles.] *I heard one of them to the effect that he had a .45 in his pocket and then heard the officer order the men against the wall, and then I was noticed and ordered likewise to stand with the others….I heard the officer order the four and myself to put your hands up and then listened to the tallest one* [later identified as Charles Ferguson] *tell the officer that he had a .45 in his pocket and reach toward a pocket with his left hand and was calling the officer numerous names. The shortest one* [later identified as Alphonso] *seemed he wanted to fight the officer. The officer fired his gun, and the shortest one rushed forward and was struck by one of the shots.*

When asked if he knew the Ferguson brothers, Crummell stated that he had "known them most of his life, about eighteen years, and had been 'friendly' with them." (Crummell most likely befriended Alphonso during their employment at the Texas Ranger.) Crummell further detailed that he sent cigarettes to Alphonso in jail.

During the questioning, Chief Elar told Crummell, "I don't want to rough it up with you fellows, but Charles hollered that he had a .45 and reached in his pocket." Crummell responded, "I would have conducted myself in the same manner if I was a police officer."[71]

Of all the statements given on the morning of February 5, Officer Joseph Romeika's was the shortest. Most of the statements lasted more than twenty minutes, but Romeika's was ten minutes, between the time of 3:32 a.m. and 3:42 a.m. District Attorney Gulotta conducted the questioning. It was witnessed by Captain Stuyvesant Pinnell, Sergeant Henry Koehl, Lieutenant Marcel Chagnon, and Chief Elar of the Freeport Police Department and recorded by Nathan Birchall.

Romeika stated:

> *While walking from the front of the building, one of the four said, "You fucking white cop: we ain't afraid of you." In response, I inquired about the trouble, and the brothers said, "We just don't like no fucking white cops, you bitch." I then said, shut up, where are you going, and they replied, "what the fuck business is that of yours: we can fix your wagon right now." The men approached me, and I kicked one in the belly, shoved the other, and then drew my gun. I ordered the men against the wall, went to the call box, and called Lieutenant Dixon on the front desk while my gun was pointed.* [Later in the statement, Romeika said that while making the call to Dixon, he ordered the men to walk to the pole with him and, after his call, ordered them to line up against the wall.] *On the call to Dixon, I requested a patrol wagon, and the men said, "You better not walk the streets of Bennington Park no more; we are going to fix you, you fucking white bastard." Another negro approached the men, and I ordered him to stand against the wall. They said, "You fucking white cop, you ain't going to take us to jail." I replied, yes, you are going to jail; stand right there.*
>
> *Charles, the older one, seemed to do most of the yelling, and he said, "You fucking white bastard, I am going to kill you right now." I said yeah, and then Charles said I got a .45 and lowered his hands. I ordered him to take his hands away from his pocket; he said fuck you, and another negro tried to grab my gun, saying, "We ain't afraid of your gun either, you*

> *bastard." At this time, I fired two shots at Charles and the second at the person that tried to grab the gun.*

Romeika further explained that Crummell, lined up against the wall with the four brothers, said, "Officer, I know these men, but I saw the way he reached for his gun, and I will be your witness. I saw the way he attempted to kill you, and I will be your witness. These men are no friends of mine or anything." Romeika then stated that he believed the brothers had been drinking based on their appearance but did not believe they were drunk. Further, in his statement, Romeika recalled that he had just investigated a burglary and rifling of a cash register that occurred shortly before the shooting and was perpetrated by a Black person about one block from where he shot the brothers.

In custody, Joseph had an officer apply a strip of adhesive tape to his gunshot wound in his shoulder. The stenographer was Nathan Birchall. Joseph was held in a holding cell until 4:28 a.m., when District Attorney Frank Gulotta interrogated him with Freeport police captain Stuyvesant Pinnell, Lieutenant Marcel Chagnon, Chief Peter Elar, and Sergeant Henry Koehl. Joseph told the officers, "I do not feel good," during the interrogation. His recollection of the chain of events was not clear.

Joseph stated:

> [We] *left his home and went to Hempstead but could not remember the names of the places* [we] *drank beer. We drank approximately four beers at the first stop, and in the second place,* [we] *drank three beers each. Then* [we] *went back to where* [we] *first went and drank two more beers. Then took a bus back to Freeport and went to a restaurant at the bus terminal and was told there was no coffee.... Words were exchanged between us* [and] *the proprietor. Charles took off his coat during the argument, and there was loud arguing and hollering. Richard and I held Charles back to prevent him from attacking the proprietor.* [We] *took Charles out of the restaurant, went to The Nest, and might have had a few beers each. Because* [we] *got into an argument,* [we] *were told to leave The Nest and walk back toward the terminal.* [Joseph described himself as feeling all right, but Charles was a little ricky or scrappy.] [I] *think maybe Charles could have broken the window, but* [we] *encountered a police officer, and an argument ensued as* [we] *walked. The officer kicked Charles in the groin, and I was kicked in the hip. We then were backed against the wall. Charles then told the officer, "Is this the right thing? You get home on leave, and cops want to lock you up." Then I heard Charles say, "I have a .45," and his hands were lowered, and then I heard the shots.*[72]

The integration concluded around 4:55 a.m. A little later in the morning, U.S. Navy lieutenant Fred Frey took Joseph into custody and treated his gunshot wound.

After seeing three of his brothers shot, two dying from their injuries, Richard was interrogated from 3:47 a.m. to 4:22 a.m. by Assistant District Attorney Frank A. Gulotta. Richard, unlike Joseph, did not have the significant presence of Freeport police officers while being questioned. During questioning, Richard was more combative in his answering of the questions.

Like his brother Joseph, Richard stated that the brothers left their home around 9:00 p.m. for Hempstead, went to Eddie's in Hempstead, and had three or four beers. But unlike his brother's recollection of the events, Richard said they went to The Nest first around midnight, might have had several beers, and then went to the terminal for coffee after leaving The Nest. Aligning with Joseph's statement, Gus refused them coffee, which started an argument, and Charles began to "peel his clothes off to fight." Charles was restrained, and they walked back to The Nest for more beers. They returned from The Nest and walked toward the terminal, meeting Officer Romeika. Charles and Romeika started arguing; Richard was standing on the right side and Charles on the left. Richard stated that he was five to ten feet away from Charles and the officer and could not hear the conversation due to heavy wind gusts (the morning weather was twenty-two degrees, with winds gusting at thirteen miles per hour). Romeika kicked Charles in the groin and told them to put their hands up. Then Richard heard two shots.[73]

When asked if he heard Charles say he had a gun, Richard said that he did not but noted that his hearing was limited because of the wind. When asked if Charles was moving his hands to his pockets after being told to put his hands up, Richard stated that he did not recall.

Following the statements of the witnesses at the station, Chief Elar decided not to suspend Romeika. Elar shared his decision not to suspend Romeika with Assistant District Attorney Gulotta, who did not express an objection. Later in statements in front of a state commission, Elar said, "I will not suspend a man doing his duty."[74]

At 10:00 a.m., Richard was on trial for disorderly conduct in the Freeport Village Police Court, with Judge Hilbert Johnson presiding over the case. Richard pleaded not guilty, but he was not given a lawyer or granted an adjournment during the brief proceedings. No district attorney was present, and the judge conducted all direct questioning. Court transcripts are cited directly from Village of Freeport Police Court records.

The four witnesses called in the testimony against Richard included Joseph Romeika, Herman Crummell, George Couloras, and Gus Cholakis. The first person called to testify was Romeika, who stated:

> *Richard was in the company of the other three defendants. I just resumed patrol over at signal box 14 on Henry Street when Gus Cholakis, proprietor of the Terminal Tea Room, said four men threatened him and broke the Sinclair's Coal Company window. The four defendants approached me using abusive language as I investigated the window. Most of the profane language was said by Charles, but Richard backed him up on every count. I then arrested the four for disorderly conduct and called Lt. Dixon from box 14 for a wagon. I told them to line up by the wall, and they said, "We will kill you," and called me a "white bastard." Gus later identified them as the ones that broke the window.*

Before the judge dismissed Romeika from the stand, he asked Richard if he had any questions for him, and Richard told the judge no. The following person called to the stand was Gus Cholakis, who stated:

> *I was closing up around 12:40, and the defendants came in. I think they are all brothers. They asked for coffee, and I said I had no coffee; but offered them tea or cocoa, but they insisted on coffee. I started to get scared and told them to leave, but they refused to leave. The fellow that got shot asked me for coffee, and all together started to put up a fight and called me names. All four called me names and were knocking me. One of them jumped at me, and the other three held him down. Fifteen minutes later, they pulled the one out trying to jump at me, and I locked the door. From the door window, about 200 to 300 feet away, I saw them break the window. Unsure as to which of the four. When I saw the officer, I reported the incident. Later I saw the fellows returning, and the officer gathered them together. I started to finish cleaning up around the shop, and then I heard two shots. I was afraid the four brothers had killed the cop. I called up that four colored guys had attacked a policeman, and I heard two shots.*

The judge then asked Cholakis, "Is your friend here? Who was in the shop at the time?" Chokakis replied yes. The following person called was George Couloras, who stated:

> *I was in a booth reading my newspaper and heard the brothers come in and ask for coffee. Gus said he had no more coffee and offered them tea or*

cocoa. He was getting ready to close. He was then threatened with all kinds of language. They called him a bitch and other things. The four were told to leave but did not go. One time one defendant pushed another guy and tried to get him out. He refused to go and started to go behind the counter. They pulled the other defendant out, and all four walked down by the coal company. Cholakis saw the officer and told him of the events. I later heard two shots and saw two fellows on the floor and the others with hands raised.

After asking Richard if he had any questions for the witness, Richard said no. Herman Crummell was called next:

I didn't see the window being broken. I was returning from the Texas Rangers, helping my father, who works there. I was leaving the Ranger's back door to the bus terminal. When I got closer to the terminal, the cop said, "You get the fuck against the wall." I was on the wall too, and I heard curse words.

He was asked if the defendant, Richard, said the curses. Crummell said, "No, I do not know who." The judge asked Richard if he had questions for Crummell, and Richard replied that he did not. Richard was then asked to take the stand.

On the stand, Richard was asked by Judge Johnson in direct examination, "Will you tell us what happened on February 5, 1946, on Henry Street?"

Richard: As they said, Charles, Joseph, and Alphonso came down to Freeport and went to Gus's Tea Room. And just like what was said, he didn't have coffee. I was willing to let it go, but my brother Charles insisted on having coffee. And they started passing words back and forth, and Joseph grabbed Charles to take him outside. We got him out; there were no blows. When we came back through the Bus Terminal, the officer kicked my brother and ordered us against the wall by the coal place.

Judge Johnson: Anyone break any windows?

Richard: No.

Judge Johnson: No broken windows in Raynor's Coal Yard?

Richard: I think that happened when we came out of Gus's.

Judge: Do you remember that?

Richard: Yes.

Judge Johnson: You all broke the window?

Richard: Yes, I guess so…I don't know….

Judge Johnson: Do you remember some of the languages stated here used by the four of you?

Richard: My brother said some as we were in a group talking. We were talking among ourselves coming up from The Nest. You know when a bunch of guys get together and get talking.

Judge Johnson: You were not among yourselves when you stated that you weren't afraid of cops?

Richard: I don't recall anyone saying that. And do not recall what was said. No profane language was spoken to the officer.

Judge Johnson: You were polite to him?

Richard: No, but we weren't cursing at him. At least I wasn't. I did not say a word to him.

Judge Johnson: Was any profane language used in the restaurant [Terminal Tea Room]*?*

Richard: I think my older brother [Charles] *was cursing.*

Judge Johnson: Did you hear testimony that you had used some?

Richard: I did not curse in Gus's.

Judge Johnson: You were with your three brothers when they went into the restaurant, and when asked to leave for at least fifteen minutes, you refused to leave?

Richard: I wanted to go, but my older brother kept at Gus, and we tried to bring him outside. I would have gone about my business.

Judge Johnson: You didn't go, though? You take such good care of your brother that someone broke the window?

Richard: Yes.

Judge Johnson: When the officer refers to the language used—you were a perfect gentleman? Didn't you hear any profane language used in the officer's presence?

Richard: No.

Judge Johnson: At all times, I assume—or shall I say—how far you were from any three brothers at any time?

Richard: About seven to eight feet.

Judge Johnson: You were all together?

Richard: Yes.

Judge Johnson: You want me to believe that if you were within eight feet of your brothers all the time, the officer isn't telling the truth?

Richard: No, I didn't say that.

Judge Johnson: You aren't hard of hearing?

Richard: No.

The judge then asked if Richard had anything to add and reminded him that it was within his right.

Despite the multiple eyewitness testimonies taken by police of an officer who gunned down two unarmed men, Richard was found guilty. The judge never questioned the officer's actions or examined the events that led to the two brothers being killed. In addition to being traumatized from witnessing his brothers' deaths, Richard had no legal representation and was not made aware of his rights. He was found guilty. Richard was sentenced to one hundred days in prison and a $100 fine. Judge Johnson, at the sentencing, stated, "I am not going to stand for rowdiness in this village. Four fellows going out looking for trouble will get what they want. And I want to commend any police officer who can keep trouble away from this village. When you go out looking for trouble, you usually find it. But you know, you have to stand at fault for the company you keep. The company evidently was not so good."[75]

Before being elected village justice decades earlier, the judge, Hilbert Johnson, was a village trustee in the pro-Klan political organization and the Citizens Party. In addition to serving office under a Klan-affiliated party, Johnson was a captain of the Freeport Fire Department Patriot Hose Company No. 4, which allowed Klan meetings in the company building and sponsored the annual Klan Cup Fireman races. Johnson was the same judge who had dropped the Ernest Louis kidnapping charges against Klan member Travis Parker decades earlier. These connections could well have influenced his ruling on Richard's sentence.

Chapter 9

FEBRUARY 6 AND THE DAYS TO COME

The late edition of *Newsday*'s headlines on February 5 read, "3 Brothers Shot in Freeport: 1 Dies." Initial news coverage of the event reported the shooting as the climactic result of disorderliness and threats in the Freeport Bus Terminal, culminating in a self-defense killing by a Freeport Village cop. Romeika was not suspended, nor was his decision to use lethal force initially investigated. District Attorney James Gehrig's office told *Newsday*, "Romeika will come before the Grand Jury next Tuesday, as a routine case, but Romeika acting in the line of duty was unquestionably justified." The authorities did not release the death of Alphonso for almost a day. The only information released to local reporters was that his condition was "very poor" and that he remained hospitalized at Meadowbrook Hospital.

A few days following the shooting, Charles R. Ferguson was buried at the Long Island National Cemetery with full military honors. As he was lowered into the ground, Charles's widow, Minnie, and his three children stood sobbing, inconsolable by neighbors in their community of Roosevelt. Less than twenty miles away, west of the Long Island National Cemetery, Alphonso was buried at Greenfield Cemetery in Uniondale.

On February 7, an organized local delegation descended on the Freeport Police Department to confront Chief Peter Elar. The delegation included Reverend Theodore Bobilin of Mineola Methodist Church, Reverend Frederick Meyer of the Rockville Centre Congregational Church, Reverend Wesley Haines of First Baptist Church, Bertram Alves of the Negro Veterans

Left: Charles Ferguson's grave at Pinelawn Cemetery. *Courtesy of Christopher Verga.*

Right: Charles's widow, Minnie, and their three sons (*left to right*), Charles, Wilfred, and Richard, following the burial. *Courtesy of Wilfred Ferguson.*

Organization, Richard Sanders of the United Veterans for Equality, Blandena Lee of the NAACP (the same Blandena Lee involved in the legal action against the Franklin Square Grill), Margert Watt and Alexander Coleman with the American Labor Party, and twenty-four other concerned community members. The delegation petitioned that Romeika be suspended pending an investigation into the shooting.[76] Chief Elar stated that the case was closed, and the delegation should take their requests to the District Attorney's Office and Mayor Cyril Ryan. The Ferguson family met and retained lawyer Stanley Faulkner the following day. Acquainted with the family, Richard Sanders was asked to introduce Faulkner after being contacted by community activist Margaret Watts, who convinced Faulkner to take the case free of charge. Faulkner began working immediately to have Richard's conviction overturned or get a retrial.

One of the first people Faulkner interviewed was Joseph Ferguson. Faulkner went to the Lido Beach Navy separation center and arranged with navy lieutenant Fred Frey to get Joseph from the brig for an interview. Once Joseph was retrieved and in front of Faulkner, Joseph said, "Do you see this coat I have on? There is a hole. This is the same coat I was wearing that night—It went right through my shoulder and came through the other side."[77] He recounted his story clearly but was still in a volatile emotional state.

This page: The NAACP, local veterans' groups, and concerned citizens at Freeport Village court meeting with Chief Elar, expressing concerns over the shooting. *Courtesy of Freeport Historical Society.*

Following Joseph's interview, Faulkner met with Richard to get his account. Faulkner summarized his interview with Richard in a statement to *Newsday*: "Everything happened so fast between the time Richard saw one of his brothers killed and the trial, several hours later, that Richard doesn't have a complete understanding of what took place in court. Richard could not adequately defend himself with which the speed of the trial was ordered."[78] A week later, Faulkner's calls for Richard's conviction to be overturned evolved into calls for justice in the murders of Charles and Alphonso. At a rally, dozens of people crowded into 56 West Merrick Road, Freeport, to express their concerns to state assemblyman Hulan Jack. Demands included the governor appointing a special prosecutor to investigate the shooting and any hearing relating to the case before a grand jury.[79] In response to the delegation demanding justice, District Attorney James Gehrig told the *Nassau Daily Review Star*, "I feel if the men shot were White, there would have been no issue here. It is a shame that the color question has to be raised." Under the growing criticism about how Gehrig's office handled the case and his personal views, a grand jury convened to decide whether to indict Romeika for the murders of the Ferguson brothers. The all-white grand jury comprised five women and sixteen men; the presiding judge was Justice Cortland A. Johnson.

On February 11, a grand jury heard the case presented by Gehrig. At the hearing, Edward Ferguson, the fifth brother, who lived in Washington, D.C., was accompanied by Selma Rose, a longtime neighbor of the family. Speaking to whoever would listen but hoping to get the district attorney's attention, Rose pointed to Edward's cut leather waistcoat and stated, "That's the kind of jacket that Charles wore that night. If anyone carried a gun under such a jacket, it would be quite obvious to a policeman."[80]

Faulkner, the family attorney and lawyer for the newly formed Citizens Committee for Justice in the Ferguson Case gave the district attorney two witnesses: Madeline Moher and Joan Vollmer. Both women testified to the "good conduct of the four brothers before entering the tea room and how they were refused coffee by Gus [Cholakis] even while white patrons were served coffee." The following day, Faulkner gave the witness statements of Arthur Stevenson, who witnessed the shooting, and said that he saw the brothers lined up against the wall and did not witness anything that would "justify the shooting." In response to Faulkner's request, Stevenson and Moher's statements were formally taken on February 13 by District Attorney James Gehrig in his office.

Arthur Stevenson, who was at the bus terminal during the shooting, said:

> [I] *observed the police officer who had four* [he did not see Crummell approach the men or line up against the wall] *of the men of color lined up against the little building. The officer told them to "stick them up, and if you don't, I will plug you."* [I] *did not hear Charles say he had a .45 but did observe one of the men of color put his hands down, but the officer made him put his hands up again....* [I] *could not tell if they were of color, did not hear anything, or see the officer kick one of the men. After the first man was shot* [Charles], *the officer whirled around and shot the shorter man* [Alphonso], *who had his hands up.* [I] *did not observe the shorter man attempt to approach the officer.*[81]

District Attorney James Gehrig questioned Madeline Moher, with daughter Joan present, and Charles Koener was the appointed stenographer. Moher's initial statement differed slightly from the Ferguson family's lawyer's interviews with Moher. Moher stated:

> [I] *was returning home from Mineola to Freeport and saw the brothers on the bus in Hempstead to Freeport.* [My] *impression was that they had been drinking based on how they were acting but not causing any disturbance....* [I] *usually catch the bus from the terminal to* [my] *house, but the next bus was at 12:40; the last bus. While waiting,* [I] *had coffee at the terminal coffee/tearoom with* [my] *daughter. When* [we] *finished* [our] *coffees,* [we] *witnessed the four brothers come in for coffee.* [I] *heard no arguing, and the brothers left before* [we] *left.*

Following the submission of the two statements of Moher and Stevens, Theodore Curphey, the Nassau County medical examiner, was called to testify. Curphey performed the autopsies of Alphonso and Charles. He testified that Charles was dressed in his U.S. Army uniform with the marks of a private first class. The "bullet wound at just about the junction of the breastplate with the clavicle. This entry wound was 55 inches from the left heel and 51 inches exit wound from the left heel. The wound included a laceration of the lung and the aorta." Curphey also testified that the alcohol level of Charles was 0.2 percent, which was consistent with someone not intoxicated (based on the measure at the time). When directed to explain the autopsy results for Alphonso, Curphey stated, "Alphonso was in civilian clothes, and the bullet entered the frontal area, above the right eye, lodging in his skull. The bullet upon entry caused laceration of the brain and hemorrhage." The alcoholic level on the brain was hard to measure due to his spending more than seven hours in the hospital, and Curphey stated that he "would not want to speculate of the alcoholic levels of the brain at the time he was shot." The following person to testify was Walter Mallory Scherdt, the ambulance driver. Scherdt testified that "two men were lying on the ground—one had a sheet over him and was advised that he was pronounced dead. Another man was lying on his left side with a bullet hole in his forehead on the left side. He was still alive and was rushed to Meadowbrook Hospital and died about 7 to 8 hours later." George Graham, an intern at the hospital, was then called, and he testified that he declared Alphonso dead at 10:12 a.m. on February 5.

On February 13, Faulkner requested that Joseph Ferguson testify before the grand jury. In custody on February 5 after the shooting, Joseph had witnessed his brothers shot and was suffering from an untreated gunshot wound. Due to these factors, Joseph's initial statement could have been given out of fear or desperation. During the grand jury hearing, District Attorney James Gehrig did not focus on the weaknesses in Joseph Ferguson's initial statement on February 5.

On the stand, Joseph stated:

> *After leaving The Nest,* [we] *went back to the bus station to go home. Charles and Alphonso walked in front, Richard and myself behind. Charles was swearing but did not hear the conversation as* [we] *were walking because I was 25 feet behind. The cop was in front of Charles. The cop was standing near the police phone on the pole and had just finished telephoning at that time. Charles might have attempted to strike the officer when the officer kicked him. I do not know. Richard and I walked up to the group. We wanted to know what was going on. When Charles and I were kicked, the officer drew his gun. He ordered us against the wall and used the telephone to call the police wagon. Charles cursed at the officer and said he might have a .45, as his and our hands were in the air. Charles slowly lowered his right hand near his hip. Then the officer fired, Charles fell, and on the second shot, Alphonso fell. Alphonso did not try to grab the cop. I did not see Alphonso move and was way off the other brothers by 12 to 15 feet. Before all this happened, Crummell came along and was lined up against the wall.*

When asked by Gehrig if he had moved from his position, Joseph replied that he "did not move from his position and the bullet went through me into Alphonso, who was behind me. The bullet went through my muscle, from my right shoulder to Alphonso standing behind me. Richard stood still the whole time. Our hands were up in the air the whole time, and we did not know why the officer fired a second time. Charles had no revolver or ever carried a revolver."

Gehrig then asked Joseph about Charles's criminal record; Joseph replied that Charles was convicted of attempted burglary. Gehrig then asked about Alphonso, to which Joseph replied that he was convicted of disorderly conduct. When asked about Richard, Joseph said he was convicted of statutory rape.

The following person called to the stand was Richard Ferguson. Richard stated:

> *On the way back from The Nest, Charles and Alphonso walked in front and Joseph and I in the back. When we reached the coal office where the window was broken, Charles and the officer talked, and I did not hear the conversation. The next thing was the officer kicking Charles in the groin, reaching for his gun, and ordering him against the wall. I did not hear swearing between Charles and the cop. I did not see Charles try to hit the cop, and I was 10 feet away. Charles and the officer were close together.*

When asked by Gehrig again if he heard Charles call the officer a white bastard and try to strike him, Richard replied, "I did not hear cursing or see Charles try to hit him."

Richard continued:

> *The officer and Charles were arguing now, and I did not know what they were saying. When Charles drinks, he is not a nice guy but friendly when he does not drink. The officer did make a call, but the officer at no point said* [we] *were under arrest. During the arguing, Crummell walked up, and the officer told him to stand along with the others. Then I heard the shots. I did not hear Charles say he had a gun, a .45. Charles, during this time, was argumentative but not drunk. I did not see the first shot; the second shot was aimed at Joseph. The officer moved in front of Joseph and deliberately fired a shot. All the rest of us had our hands in the air at the time of the second shot. I did not hear anything about a .45; I have very good hearing.*

Gehrig then asked Richard to repeat the story, and Richard repeated his account. When asked about the last time he spoke to his brother Joseph, Richard replied, "I have not seen Joseph since the morning of the Freeport Court hearing, have not spoken to him since last Wednesday."

When asked if anyone advised him before testifying in front of the grand jury and if he retained Faulkner as a lawyer, Richard stated, "No one advised me before appearing in front of the jury. I am represented by Mr. Faulkner, whom I did not engage [his family retained Faulkner for Richard's defense]. I do not know who engaged him for me. Mr. Faulkner never told me. I saw Charles's wife, and she gave me the papers, stating that he was a lawyer. I have requested the money for the fine from my aunt, and I have no more for a lawyer."

In closing, Gehrig asked about his criminal record. Richard said that he "pled guilty to statutory rape. The girl had a child, and I pay child support."

Next to be called was Herman Crummell, who stated:

> *About 1:30, I was passing the bus terminal in Freeport. As I was approaching Henry street, one of the Ferguson brothers called me over; I do not remember which one. They were talking with the cop on the side of the building. The cop asked what the trouble was. They started cursing and using bad language. Charles was the worst with cursing. They said, "No white cop son of a bitch is going to lock us up." Alphonso kept the ball rolling by saying, "Damn you, you ain't going to lock us up." The cop then said they were under arrest. The cop told us to keep our hands up and made us line up against the wall. The cop then made a phone call.*

When asked if the Romeika kicked Charles, Crummell added, "I did not see the cop kick Charles in the groin at any time. The cop told them to put their hands up." He continued, "Then Charles hollered he had a .45. Charles went to put his hands down, and the cop made him put his hands up again. Alphonso tried to rush the cop, and the cop shot him. This was after Charles got shot. Alphonso ran out of line and dropped his hands—his left hand."

When asked where the brothers were standing, Crummell replied, "At the corner, Charlie was first, then Richard, then Alphonso, then Joseph. Charles was on this side of Joseph, which is the right side. The same hand that dropped towards his pocket." Crummell was asked if Romeika said anything after the shooting. He replied, "The officer said nothing to me except that he wanted a witness." Crummell continued, "Charles dropped as soon as he was hit, staggering about two feet, and then fell at the corner of the building. I do not know if the cop stayed in the same place when he shot the second time and do not know how Joseph got shot."

Next to testify on the stand was Officer Joseph Romeika. Before the testimony, it was clarified that he had signed a waiver of immunity, so anything he said could be used against him. Romeika recounted:

> *At midnight, I was on foot patrol and assigned to investigate a burglary, but resumed my normal patrol at 1:25 a.m. I was called by Gus Cholakis, who told me four men of color threatened to kill him with a .45. Gus explained they wanted coffee but had none and offered them tea and cocoa. They insisted on coffee and threatened to shoot him and left, breaking the window of the Sinclair Coal Company....I rang the police phone, resumed my patrol, and walked to the coal company. The four men of color approached me. One of them said, "Fucking cop, we ain't afraid of you." I asked them what the trouble was, and they said, "We don't like any fucking white cop." I told them to shut up, and the four came at me. I shoved one of them back and drew my gun. I told them they were under arrest and to put up their hands. I marched them back to the signal box. I called the desk officer Dixon to send a wagon. I have four prisoners. After I hung up, I had them march to the coal company wall and told them to stay there....They were using abusive language; when Crummell came along, he asked them what the trouble was. They told him this white mother fucker cop and white bastard wants to lock them up. I then lined Crummell up against the wall with the others. While standing there, Charles said, "You ain't going to lock us up." I said I am; the pie wagon is on the way down. Charles said he got a .45 in his back pocket and will kill me. I said, keep your hands up. Charles then called me a white bastard and said he would kill me. Charles reached for his assumed .45. I gave it to him—gave it to him as the other one came at me.*

When probed to further elaborate, Romeika added, "The men were lined up at my right side—Herman, Charles, Joseph, Richard, and Alphonso. Alphonso was to my left. I fired from my waistline. I shot Charles first and then shot Alphonso." When asked about why and where Alphonso was at the time he was shot, Romeika stated, "I shot him [Alphonso] as he was reaching for my gun. Alphonso did not step out and then back; he lunged and tried to grab my gun. He came running, and he took a rush at my gun, and that is when I shot him." He was then asked if he intended to injure or kill them; Romeika responded, "I had no intention to shoot to kill." Romeika was asked about the level of danger and if Joseph was a threat. Romeika stated, "I was about eight feet from Charles when I shot him. I had no way of knowing whether Charles had a gun or not. I do not recall if Joseph made a move toward me. I kept looking to my back to make sure no Negro would jump me from the back." When asked about Joseph being shot, Romeika replied, "There is a possibility that the bullet ricocheted off the wall and hit the sailor [Joseph]." In closing, Romeika confirmed that he had never been forced to pull his gun before and was not interviewed by Faulkner.

While questioning witnesses Madeline Moher and reviewing her statement on February 13, Gehrig emphasized her trade union affiliation with the Congress of Industrial Organizations (CIO). Gehrig questioned her on her union affiliations and asked if they might conflict with her testimony. Later, when asked about Gehrig's cross-examination, Moher stated; "The impression I got from the district attorney was he had more interest in conveying to the Grand Jury the facts of my work, organizations I belong to, and organizations that the attorney for the Ferguson family belongs to—instead of the shooting deaths of two persons and the wounded third."[82]

Arthur Stevenson was called to the stand to elaborate on his statement on February 13. Stevenson stated:

> *I live in Roosevelt but do not know the Ferguson brothers….I was taking the bus home and was at the Freeport bus terminal. Across from the terminal,* [I] *saw and heard the officer bring the men down, telling them to get over there and stick them up and keep them up, and if they didn't, he would plug them. He went to the phone box, telephoned, and told them to keep them up….The cop walked back to the colored men. I saw one of the men fall—the tallest one* [Charles]. *I heard the shot. I heard one more shot and saw another man fall. I did not see the tall one* [Charles] *lower his hands. I saw the little one [Alphonso] step out of line but get back in line. I did not know if any of them put their hands down. What I saw was them with their hands still up. My vision was partly obscured. I did not see the big one lower his hands. I only saw four against the wall, not five. I know Crummell but didn't see him. I saw the officer shoot one of them while his hands were up.*

When asked how he learned that Crummell was there that night, Stevenson noted, "Crummell once told [me] what happened, and that was the first time I knew Crummell was there. In my conversation with Crummell, he did not say that Alphonso had tried to grab the gun of the cop or run at him." Stevenson replied when asked how Faulkner got his statement, "I didn't tell the police. I gave my account to Faulkner. I contacted Faulkner, and he came to my house, and Crummell might have given him the address."

On the final days of the grand jury hearing, Gehrig subpoenaed Ferguson's family lawyer Faulkner to take the stand. Gehrig's questions were not related to the shooting. Instead, they were centered on Faulkner's membership in the Lawyers Guild, his work with CIO unions, and possible communist affiliation. The questions then shifted to what relationship Faulkner had with the Citizens Committee. Faulkner was the last of the witnesses called to testify before the grand jury deliberated.

As the grand jury hearing played out, details were reported daily to the media that stirred up reactions. At the annual dinner of the National Conference of Christians and Jewish People at the Garden City Hotel, a collective appeal was made for justice. It demanded a war against oppression that had to start in Nassau County. Gehrig was invited and in attendance but left at the beginning of Rabbi Roland Gittelsohn's speech on the pending case. Rabbi Gittelsohn stated, "I do not have all the facts, and I don't believe anyone does, but I am positive that if the four brothers had been white men, they'd be alive today. We haven't the moral right to meet in the name of brotherhood unless we mean it. If the opposite is true in one of our communities, something should be done about it."[83] Other fellowship leaders referenced the injustice of the Ferguson brothers and asserted that structural biases kept the Freeport community of color in substandard housing.

A few miles away from the Garden City Hotel, in the courtroom, tactics of red-baiting witnesses became a typical attempt to divert the central debate away from the shooting and the flawed system of justice in the county. But the growing discussion on institutional racism got the attention of various labor groups and local chapters of the Communist Party, which started organizing rallies to support justice for the Ferguson family, further focusing the debate on communist influence within the community. The Communist Party of New York State met on how to best manage a campaign for justice on February 21 at the Odd Fellows Hall of Hempstead. Benjamin Davis, New York City councilman, was the keynote speaker during the rally. Davis, in a passionate joint statement with an officer of the state Communist Party, Charles Loman, declared:

> *The spirit of Hitler is alive in Freeport. The Fascist filibuster tactics of the Bilbos* [referring to Mississippi governor Theodore Bilbo, an open Ku Klux Klan member] *and Eastlands in the U.S. Senate and the propaganda of fascist groups are encouraging lynchers and anti-Semites all over America. We protest and denounce this lynch attack upon innocent negro citizens. The Communist Party calls upon the people of New York State to declare their abhorrence of this bloody deed. We call on the people to demand the removal of patrolman Romeika and his trial for manslaughter. We demand the release of Richard Ferguson from the Nassau County Jail and indemnity for the slain brothers.*[84]

In the midst of the groups calling for justice, Joseph Ferguson was cleared of misconduct charges by the U.S. Navy. In a statement to *Newsday*, his commanding officer stated, "The evidence now available clearly shows that Ferguson, finding himself in a challenging position, conducted himself in a manner which in no way can be construed as misconduct." On February 21, the navy restored Joseph to full active duty.

During the closing days of the grand jury testimonies, Faulkner asked for more time to get witnesses for the hearing. All of Faulkner's requests were rejected. In reaction to Gehrig's refusals to allow more time, Minnie, Charles's widow, wrote a letter to the jury foreman pleading for a postponement of deliberation. Writing on Tuskegee Army Air Field stationery, Minnie noted that "more time was needed to gather evidence and witnesses. I request this so that justice may be done for a father of three children. A postponement would be granted to any white man in the same circumstances and should not be refused for a negro soldier."[85] Despite the pleas to find more witnesses, the jury went into deliberation.

Following the news of Joseph's acquittal by the navy of any wrongdoing, the Nassau County Grand Jury returned from deliberation at 4:30 p.m. on February 21. The jury voted not to indict Romeika on any charges. In a statement to *Newsday*, District Attorney Gehrig said, "The Grand Jury was expected to pass on whether or not the cop was justified in the action he took. In dismissing the charges, it is assumed that they believe he was justified."[86] Criticism of the verdict was almost instantaneous. Religious fellowship groups and the Citizens Committee wanted answers about "why there were no negros on the jury selected to hear the case." Addressing the case and the questions from the Citizens Committee to reporters at the annual Freeport Police Benevolent Association dinner, Gehrig stated, "A negro should have been a member of the jury, and only recently a negro served on a jury before Supreme Court Justice Courtland Johnson. In the future, I will see to it there will be members of the Grand Jury who are colored." Gehrig elaborated, "As far as justice in Nassau County is concerned, we don't have a different brand for colored or white, veteran or civilian or policeman. We will have no law enforcement officer wait until they are shot before they use their defense."[87]

Following the verdict and Gehrig's public remarks, Faulkner organized various social justice groups that supported the Ferguson family to unify behind a shared set of guiding ideas and reach out to other like-minded organizations for support. In a telegram that urged Governor Dewey and Attorney General Tom Clark to investigate the shooting, Faulkner got support from Arthur G. Hays, a lawyer for the Civil Liberties Union; Will Maslow, director of the American Jewish Congress; Paul O'Dwyer, brother of New York City mayor Thomas O'Dwyer; Abraham Unger, executive secretary of the New York City Chapter of the National Lawyers Guild; Osmond Fraenkel, national chairman of the National Lawyers Guild; and Thurgood Marshall, special counsel to the NAACP.

Further mobilizing the demands for justice was the rally Make Freeport Free. Held at the Hotel Diplomat in New York City, this rally hosted more than three hundred delegates from New York unions, American Legion posts, Veterans Against Discrimination, and local citizen groups. The groups created a shared vision and guiding principles to obtain justice for the Ferguson family. The keynote speaker was Congressman Adam Clayton Powell. Powell, in his speech, stated, "I pledge to bring the northern Scottsboro Case to the floor of Congress for a course of action." The conclusion of the rally promulgated five goals for achieving justice.

- Remove District Attorney Gehrig and establish a grand jury investigation with Governor Dewey's assistance.
- Suspend Romeika from the police force.
- Get the U.S. attorney general to proceed with a case against Romeika using state and federal civil rights law.
- Hold citywide mass meetings to protest the handling of the case.
- Get monetary assistance for the Ferguson family.[88]

While at the rally, attendee Mrs. Bradley Smith told a *Newsday* reporter, "I originally came from the south, and the conditions in Freeport will shock a southerner. We have segregated schools that the town burghers deny." Promoting the five goals of the meeting, Harry Raymond, writer for the *Daily Worker* newspaper, wrote a pamphlet called "Dixie Comes to New York: Story of Freeport GI Slayings." This pamphlet was distributed in union halls and communities of color, such as in Bennington Park. Another widely circulated pamphlet was the New York Committee for Justice in Freeport's "Scottsboro (Long Island): The Story of Murder in Freeport." This text was a more condensed account of the shooting and was only four pages, unlike the fifteen-page booklet "Dixie Comes to New York."

While civil rights and other local activist groups were organizing and planning justice campaigns, the NAACP had concerns about the Communist Party getting too involved. The local branches supported the calls for justice, but national executive secretary Walter White and

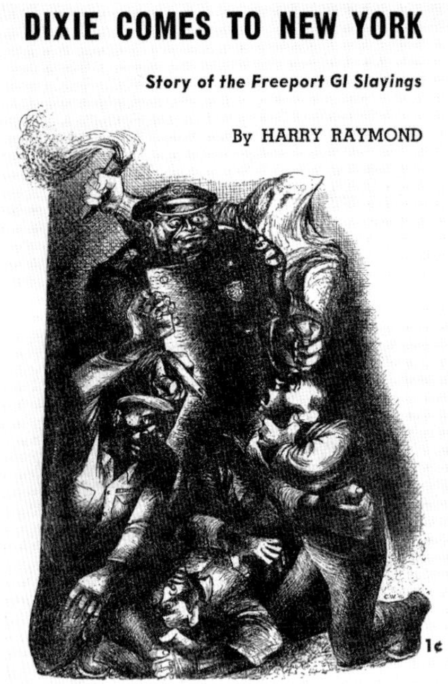

Left: The *Daily Worker*'s pamphlet "Dixie Comes to New York: Story of the Freeport GI Slayings." The pamphlet, written by Harry Raymond, provided a brief detailed account of the events of February 5. *Courtesy of the University of Rochester's Thomas Dewey Archives.*

Right: Freeport group Justice for the Ferguson Brothers created its own pamphlet, "Scottsboro (Long Island): The Story of Murder in Freeport." Similar to "Dixie Comes to New York," this pamphlet provided a brief detailed account of the events of February 5. *Courtesy of the University of Rochester's Thomas Dewey Archives.*

the organization's lawyers hesitated to advocate for justice. The NAACP lawyers were fearful that any association with the Communist Party could undermine the civil rights work of the organization and strengthen the stature of American communist groups.[89]

Throughout the entire months-long protest, the NAACP openly supported calls for a trial and prosecution by bringing Romeika up again in front of a grand jury or a state probe. As protests raged, the NAACP communicated with Governor Dewey's office to get the state to intervene. In correspondences between Governor Dewey's counsel, Charles Breitel, and NAACP special counsel Thurgood Marshall, state investigation requests were submitted as early as February 27. In his correspondences with the state, Marshall closed the letters with, "Before making any public statement based upon this memo, I would

New York's Lynching goes UNANSWERED

On FEBRUARY 5th, in Freeport, Long Island, Policeman Joseph Romeika killed Charles and Alfonzo Ferguson, wounded Joseph and arrested the fourth Ferguson brother, Richard. He acted, Romeika said, in "self defense."

When Army, Navy and then civilian authorities exonerated the brothers of any misconduct (Charles' widow received a memorial from President Truman), shocked citizens demanded investigation. In an atmosphere of race hatred, District Attorney James Gehrig of Nassau County held a Grand Jury inquiry. The result — a whitewash.

In monstrous tradition, a lynching and a legal whitewash had taken place in New York.

THE PEOPLES' ANGER organized the New York Committee for Justice in Freeport: labor, civic, veteran and religious organizations representing 2,500,000 people. They demanded that Governor Dewey act. The Governor was "busy"; he was "out of town."

On April 5th, the Ku Klux Klan entered the case with a threat letter to the Committee. The shocking fact of the Klan's legal functioning in New York, made public by the Committee, forced the Governor's hand. But Dewey's Secretary of State could find no incorporation papers for the Klan.

A reporter promptly found them. Another reporter proved that Republican County leader Horace Demarest, Commissioner of Public Vehicles of Queens, was an original incorporator of the Klan. Dewey was left no alternative. He "exposed" the Klan in a burst of publicity calculated to divert attention from the central fact that the Ferguson lynching was still unanswered.

The attempt failed. Protests mounted. A delegation headed by State Assemblymen, City Councilmen and veterans presented the written demands of 40,000 angry citizens. Dewey was forced to call a "public" hearing.

The hearing was carefully staged. Witnesses were rehearsed. The Attorney for the Ferguson family was denied the right to examine witnesses. Romeika, the killer, was accorded every courtesy. So gross was the performance that 16 organizations, interested in justice, walked out of the hearings, branding them "fraudulent."

TODAY THE NATION is staggered by the most hideous series of assaults on minority people in American history. The pattern of Freeport has spread. New Yorkers, shocked by the monstrous crimes of Southern lynchers, realize that within their own state, too, a brutal lynching is unanswered. The Empire State still reeks of the Georgia lynch rope. The Governor of New York stands branded beside Talmadge, Bilbo and Rankin.

THE PATTERN OF TERROR SPREADS

The leaflet "New York's Lynching Goes Unanswered" detailed the slow response from New York State and the rise of racial tensions from a resurgence of the Klan. *Courtesy of the University of Rochester's Thomas Dewey Archives.*

appreciate your contacting me."[90] In additional letters between local/state officials and the NAACP, they noted that "in our investigation, police exceeded their bounds necessary to quell a disturbance of the kind he was faced. This is a travesty on justice and constitutes additional threats to the community, including having the same officer [Romeika] walk the beat."[91] A memo between NAACP president Walter White and Thurgood Marshall regarding how to proceed noted that they would need "sufficient pressure to be brought to bear upon the district attorney that he will present the officer to a grand jury again."[92]

With the organized campaign for justice and the support from Congressman Adam Clayton Powell, the outcry became national, seeping into popular culture. Folk singer Woody Guthrie, disgusted over the deaths of the two Ferguson brothers and the blinding of Isaac Woodard, wrote a protest song related to the shooting. The twelve-verse song details the events of February 5, including the tea room's refusal to serve the brothers coffee. Toward the end of the song, the effects of the shooting and racial inequalities are detailed:

Let's stop here and drink us a hot cup of coffee
That Long Island bus was an awful long ride;
But we've got to keep your blood warm, our young brother, Charles,
Because you've reenlisted for quite a long time.
You've been over the ocean and won your good record
A Private First Class needs hot coffee the same
As Alonzo [Alphonso] *or Joseph or just plain old Richard*
We'll all drink a hot cup to each brother's name.
It's nice of the bus terminal to have a good tea room
Mr. Scholakis [Cholakis] *is the owner; there's his card on the wall.*
Let's sit over here and wash down our troubles,
And if you know a tall story, my brother, tell them all.
The waiter shakes his head, wipes his hands on his apron,
He says there's no coffee in all that big urn;
In that glass gauge there, it looks like several inches,
It looks like this tea room's got coffee to burn.
We gave him a speech in a quiet, friendly manner
We didn't want to scare you, ladies, over there;
He calls for a cop on his phone on the sly,
And the cop came and marched us out in the night's air.
The cop said that we had insulted the joint man.
He made us line up with our faces to the wall;
We laughed to ourselves as we stood there and listened
To the man of law and order putting in his riot call.
The cop turned around and walked back to young Charlie
Kicked him in the groin and then shot him to the ground;
This same bullet went through the brain of Alonzo
And the next bullet laid my brother Joseph down.
My fourth brother Richard got hauled to the station
Bawled out and lectured by the judge on his bench.
The judge said us Fergusons was looking for trouble;
They lugged Richard off for hundred days.
This morning two hearses roll out toward the graveyard
One hearse had Alonzo, and the other took Charles.
Charles' wife, Minnie, brings her three boy children
And friends and relatives in some old, borrowed cars.
Nobody has told these three little boys yet,
Everybody rides crying and shaking their heads.
Nobody knows quite how to make these three boys know

That Jim Crow killed Alonzo, that Charles too is dead.
The town that we ride through is not Rankin, Mississippi,
Nor Bilbo's Jim Crow town of Washington, D.C.
But it's greater New York, our most fair-minded city
In all this big land here and streets of the brave.
Who'll tell these three boys that their daddy is gone?
Who helped whip the Fascists and Nazis
Who'll tell these three sons that Jim Crow coffee has killed several thousand, the same as their dad?[93]

In the original notes on the song, Guthrie concluded the lyrics with:

True Storey, I See. Month of March Nineteen & Fortey Six
I would crawl from coast to coast, join any army marching out to battle, scrape, scrapple, or fight the race and hate to death.[94]

Legendary folk artist Woody Guthrie, disgusted with the events in Freeport, wrote the song "The Ferguson Brothers Shooting" to raise awareness of the murders. *Courtesy of the Library of Congress.*

Building on the backlash of the grand jury's decision not to indict and the growing national attention, the adjutant general of the command office in Mitchell Field, New York, investigated the shooting. Under Army Air Corps regulations, Mitchell Field investigated the shooting due to Charles being on active duty and a furlough. The conclusion was announced by Major G.A. Holliday of the Mitchell Field legal office, which "disagreed with the Nassau county's findings and recommended that they be disapproved. Legal officers' conclusion of the death of Charles occurred in the line of duty and not as a result of any misconduct."[95]

In response to the growing number of groups demanding justice for the Ferguson family, New York State officials started to assess the severity of potential social unrest and communist influence. In a letter from Charles Breitel, counsel to Governor Dewey, to Commissioner of Correction head Grant Reynolds, "the heaviest contributors to the Ferguson social justice groups, were the Communist Party, you may interpret this as you wish."[96]

A sketch of the Ferguson shootings by Woody Guthrie. *Courtesy of the Woody Guthrie Archives.*

Reynolds noted that Assemblyman Hulan Jack and Congressman Powell were vocal about justice for the Ferguson brothers and held rallies to seek reelection. Reynolds elaborated on Congressman Powell's speech regarding his inaction to a state investigation by "threatening to drive Dewey back into the same rat hole as Georgia Governor Talmage." Reynolds, a former member of the NAACP, and his service in the army as a person of color provided Dewey with the necessary insight into local civil rights struggles. Reynolds was also a loyal Republican Party member and assisted in Dewey's first presidential campaign in 1944 against Roosevelt, helping rally Black communities in support of Dewey. In 1944, Dewey later appointed Reynolds as head of the Commission of Correction.

In response to Breitel's updates on the growing justice movement, Dewey issued a court order to acquire all evidence, grand jury transcripts, and testimonies used in the Nassau County Grand Jury in early March for review. In additional letters to District Attorney Gehrig, Dewey clarified his intentions that he would be investigating the case and wanted a full report of the facts four months before he officially created a state probe.

As growing grass-roots efforts got the governor's attention, various local organizations started to denounce the calls for justice and refer to the activist groups as a threat against law enforcement that promoted un-American and lawless activities. The first among these groups to publicly support the Freeport Police Departments and the actions of Romeika was the Freeport Exchange Club. The Exchange Club was a community organization that promoted Americanism through local youth programs. In a letter to the mayor of Freeport and *Newsday*, the club stated:

> *The club denounces the unwarranted and un-American activities of certain individuals and groups in connection with the Ferguson case. We regret that lawlessness brings trouble and loss of life; club members were vigorous in denouncing those elements seeking to undermine the orderly procedure of law enforcement. We praise public officials' handling of the case and stand ready at all times to uphold those charged with the responsibility of orderly government.*[97]

Following this public stance and support for Romeika's actions, the Sons of the American Revolution Long Island Chapter sent Governor Dewey a letter praising the "unbiased handling of the Ferguson case and support for the Freeport public officials." Public support regarding handling the case influenced debates about supporting the Freeport Police Department within VFW halls across Nassau County. Arguments within the halls were summed up in this way: "[either] supports the lawless communists or support Freeport's lawful government." Many American Legion and Veterans of Foreign Wars posts attempted to withhold comment or resolutions of support for either the Ferguson family or Romeika. The National American Veterans Committee and Central Nassau Veterans chair John Weaver refused and requested all groups to issue no statements of support. In a statement, Weaver stated that "while the group wanted to be definite in their stand, they also want to be sure that the stand was of the majority of the organization."[98] Weaver also planned to invite the veterans' organization to investigate the Ferguson events with the Colored Veterans of Hempstead. But despite the requests of the national committee of veterans, all three American Legion and Veterans of Foreign Wars posts within Freeport Village declared their support of how Freeport officials and police had handled the Ferguson shootings.

Further feeding into the narrative of supporting Freeport law enforcement and denouncing any state inquiries were the public statements from New York State Assembly, Joseph P. Carlino of Long Beach. Assemblyman Carlino, in interviews with *Newsday*, stated:

> *There was no discrimination in the Ferguson Case. I would like to submit to you the respective criminal records of the Ferguson family. Charles was convicted of attempted burglary, Alphonso was twice convicted of disorderly conduct, and their mother Alma was indicted for assault in the first degree for stabbing her son Alphonso. Romeika is an abstainer from alcohol and tobacco with a spotless record in the community and attends regular mass at the Roman Catholic Church of Holy Redeemer. Alma is confined to Albion correctional. Furthermore, many prominent Nassau County people of color, citizens of high reputation, do not regard this unfortunate affair as a shocking lynch murder or trigger-happy discrimination but resent the attempt on the part of ill-informed individuals to incite racial animosities for political advantages.*[99]

Carlino's statement was not a local political opinion but reflected regional party sentiment toward the case. Carlino was the leader of the local Republican Club and worked with Leonard Hall, one of New York's most influential Republican leaders and later Republican National chairman. Hall, at the time, was serving as New York's Second District congressman, representing the community of Freeport. Hall remained silent about his thoughts on the shooting, but Carlino, who was in lockstep with his party, led many to assume that state party leaders shared his position.

In the heat of the public debate over the verdict in the case and the various organizations coming forward to announce their support, Freeport Mayor Cyril Ryan announced a finalized plan to revitalize the historic Black community of Bennington Park through the construction of a new housing project. The construction costs would be $741,000, with a large portion of the funds coming from the state housing authority. For over a decade, the village worked with various civic groups to access grants to complete sustainable housing for a large portion of Bennington Park, plagued by building and health code violations. The mayor welcomed the implementation of the proposed construction to shift the media attention away from the shooting. Finalizing the plan would come in response to the criticism of the structural racism in housing at the annual dinner of the National Conference of Christians and Jewish People the week prior. This proposal received praise from the Inter-Faith Clergy Council, which Mayor Ryan used to tout equality initiatives within Freeport and shift the Freeport Village news coverage. While the mayor laid out his plan in press conferences, the village board did not approve it but agreed to open it up for a ballot initiative for the upcoming village election. As the village election approached, many board members expressed their opposition to the plan, which led to a defeat of the proposal.[100]

As support for the proposal fell flat, media coverage of the shooting rose nationally. Supporters of the Freeport Police Department used the expanding coverage to further their argument that only communists would not support the authority of the law and that Freeport was falling victim to a communist conspiracy to create lawlessness. Local editorials debated secret communist cells within Freeport masked by social justice activism. Lawyer Edgar Hazelton met with the local telephone line workers union. He told the members that two communist cells within Long Island communities were attempting to create disorder in labor. Many argued that the communist cells were attracted by the activism from the Ferguson shootings. In an editorial in the *Nassau Daily-Review Star*, Freeport resident John Purdy stated that "outside communist agitators from out of town are creating racial hysteria by capitalizing on unfortunate events. Handing out pamphlets stamped with the Daily Workers in print to people of color in Bennington Park, representing themselves as the savior of the oppressed. These people are disciples of Stalin and refuse to accept the functions of democracy by rejecting our tribunal decisions."[101] To further try to silence social justice groups locally, the Freeport mayor started campaigning against any suspected communist elements. He denounced the flyers handed out by the various groups as promoting lawlessness. The mayor referred to groups as "communist agitators attempting to create disorder." In response to the mayor's remarks, the Freeport Committee for Justice in the Ferguson Case attempted to hold a mass meeting at the Hempstead Elks Club and invited the mayor to discuss his concerns. In response to the invitation, the mayor wrote a letter:

> *Your invitation to attend the meeting of the Freeport Committee for Justice in the Ferguson Case has been received. I shall not attend because I am instructing the Hempstead Elks Club to keep their premises closed next Sunday afternoon and denial of any such meeting. This action is taken to preserve the peace and maintain law and order. Confidential information has come to me to the effect that persons and patriotic groups are fed up with misrepresenting the facts of the case. This meeting is called for the avowed purpose of interfering with and superseding the normal processes of law in this state, intended to create an inflammatory nature designed to create disorder.*[102]

In addition to halting Elk Club Hall rentals, the mayor refused all protection from village services for the protesters. The mayor's actions led most Ferguson meetings to move to New York City, attracting more people to attend the rallies.

Freeport Mayor Cyril Ryan attempted to ban Ferguson family protests within the village and from the Hempstead Elks lounge. *Courtesy of Freeport Historical Society.*

During the growing divide between supporting local officials and the demands for justice, Richard Ferguson was still facing incarceration. After being released on a temporary certificate of reasonable doubt, Ferguson only served fourteen days of his original one-hundred-day sentence. Faulkner maintained the grounds of appeal on the excessive sentence, Richard not being mentally prepared to stand trial and the insufficient defense. Finally, on March 28, Richard's verdict was reversed, and his original $100 fine was remitted under Judge Henry A. Collins. But the celebration of this would be short-lived. Despite the court admitting that Richard was not mentally prepared for trial and did not have sufficient defense, the deaths of his two brothers were still an open-and-shut case as far as Freeport and Nassau County were concerned.

Meeting in secret and feeding on the communist hysteria and demands for civil rights, the Ku Klux Klan was organizing a comeback, rallying to counter the demands for justice in Freeport. Like the Klan of the 1920s, the reorganized Klan of Long Island maintained the same racial and ethnic biases from decades prior. It claimed that its responsibility was to protect law and order. But the Long Island Klan of the late 1940s expanded on a new target: communist ideology. The Klan argued that communists spread their influence through Freeport's "real American" communities. On April 5, 1946, the Klan announced the reorganizing of a chapter on Long Island. In a letter to one of the local citizen groups, the Klan stated that its new chapter had an influx of members because the Ferguson group meetings "are causing hundreds of real Americans to be aroused. New Klan members included 47 Freeport veterans and 1,761 Brooklyn ex-servicemen."[103] Detailed in the letter was the Klan's intentions to be at the next Ferguson rally at the Manhattan Center in midtown New York City watching and noting who was in attendance. The letter further elaborated its solid anti-communist beliefs and that people of color of Freeport were being excited and meeting with America's greatest enemy, the communists. In closing, the letter stated that Romeika and Gus Cholakis would not be eligible for membership in the Klan due to their ethnicities and religion. On April 9, following the initial letter, the Klan again confirmed to local media outlets that it would have members in attendance on the rally day.

The day of the Manhattan Center rally went off without any problems and with very little police presence. During the roll call of the delegates at the rally, the presiding officer asked if any Klan delegates were present, and no one announced themselves. Speakers at the rally included Mike Quill, a former Irish Republic Army officer and later the Transport Workers Union of America president, and Vito Marcantonio, former congressman of East Harlem. In their speeches, both men stated that their allies would not give in to the pressure of not seeking justice in Freeport and urged others not to yield. In the aftermath of the rally, labor unions held solidarity marches across Manhattan in the following months. A solidarity march of 1,500 garment workers paraded down 38th Street and 8th Avenue during the afternoon rush demanding the prosecution of Romeika. Later in the week, 500 unionized garment workers from the La Marquis Footwear Company marched, demanding justice and holding signs that read, "Democracy is in Danger."

This page and opposite: Ferguson brothers solidarity march of New York City garment workers and civil rights activists. *Courtesy of the New York Public Library Schomburg Collection.*

As public demonstrations increased, the Manhattan Center rally received more attention, and the Klan's potential threats grew. To strengthen the growing Klan chapter, the Klan filed papers to consolidate the regional branches under its current incorporation as a membership club in New York State. The New York Knights of the Ku Klux Klan was officially formed on October 30, 1925. Still, when filing the group's paperwork with the state, they were told that the Knights were never formally incorporated. Days before filing the paperwork, citizen groups supporting the Ferguson case demanded New York secretary of state Thomas Curran rescind or reject any incorporation of the Klan. In response to the inability to get the incorporation paperwork, the Klan stated that the setback was due to "a Klan expose in the press and by the NAACP, that made Curran deny the Klan or any other similar-titled organization incorporation in New York."[104]

On April 29, the Klan's original incorporation papers were discovered in the state. They initially granted a fraternity named Alpha Pi Sigma, which later renamed itself Knights and Women of the Ku Klux Klan. In this

discovery, one of the Knights and Women of the KKK's incorporators was the current Deputy Motor Vehicle commissioner, Horace Demarest. Dewy had Demarest dismissed from his post immediately following the discovery. When asked by *Newsday* reporters if he had any comment, Demarest replied that he "sponsored the incorporation of Alpha Pi Sigma, not the Klan, only as a favor to a lawyer he knew."[105] Following the discovery of the papers, state Supreme Court justice Benjamin Schreiber authorized the dissolution of the Klan. In a follow-up to the repeal, New York State attorney general Nathaniel Goldstein said, "Its principles of hate, intolerance, bigotry, and violence have no part in our American way of life."[106] Goldstein further explained that there would be additional probes into the Klan. The investigation was received with criticism from the Klan and the Ferguson groups. In a letter to *Newsday* from the leader of the justice citizen group, Dorothy Langston stated, "The state is trying to create a hullabaloo in the press regarding a campaign against the Klan to create political capital for the forthcoming elections, meanwhile resorting in the duplicity to avoid taking action in a case of outright murder of two negro residents of our state."[107] With the attention to the resurgence of the Klan in Freeport, local officials publicly said that the Klan did not exist or denied the Klan ever had a presence in the village. District Attorney Gehrig told *Newsday* and the *New*

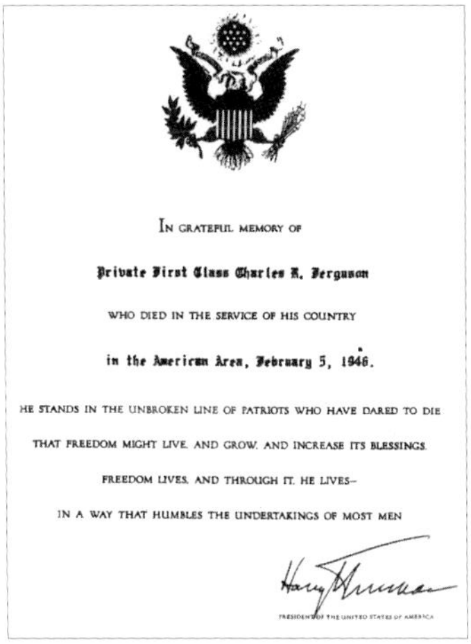

In Grateful Memory of

Private First Class Charles R. Ferguson

who died in the service of his country

in the American Area, February 5, 1946.

He stands in the unbroken line of patriots who have dared to die

that freedom might live, and grow, and increase its blessings.

Freedom lives, and through it, he lives–

in a way that humbles the undertakings of most men

President of the United States of America

Presidential citation from Harry Truman stating that Charles died in service to his country. *Courtesy of Wilfred Ferguson.*

York Times in various interviews that "there is no evidence of the Klan or revival of the Klan in Nassau County. The accusation of the Klan is not factual."

As groups continued demanding justice for the Ferguson brothers and combatting the Klan, there was a big morale boost from the federal government and the country's most famous stage actors. On May 10, 1946, Minnie Ferguson received a presidential citation for Charles's service to his country. The citation stated, "In Grateful Memory of Private First Class Charles R. Ferguson Who Died in the Service of His Country in the American Area, February 5, 1946. He Stands in the Unbroken Line of Patriots Who Have Dared to Die that Freedom Might Live, and Grow, and Increase Its Blessings. Freedom Lives, and Through It, He Lives—In a Way that Humbles the Undertakings of Most Men."

Minnie received Charles's military benefits, but processing them took time. Minnie, active in demonstrations for justice for her husband's death, strained her immediate finances. While trying to take care of her three sons, her primary source of income, from domestic work, slowed down. The media coverage of her husband's death made Minnie a spokesperson. Dorothy Langston, leader of the New York Committee for Justice in Freeport, created a trust fund to aid in the expenses for Minnie and her three sons. A champagne party was organized among some of the biggest stars on Broadway. Known Black celebrities such as singer Kenneth Spencer and Josephine Premice teamed up with Austrian refugee and seasoned theater actor Oskar Homolka to promote the party among the city's elite. "The human side of the case cannot be forgotten," Langston stated at the party of a few dozen people.[108] On the first night, $750 was raised; later, $1,500 more was donated. While promoting the human side of the case, an influx of Black actors inspired by the cause started to organize for civil rights issues to a broader audience. Following the cocktail party fundraiser, Black Broadway actor Robert Earl Jones (father of James Earl Jones) became an outspoken advocate for justice for the Ferguson family and other civil rights issues. Walter Winchell, a famous columnist and radio personality, publicly criticized the Elks Club and local officials for refusing citizen groups that advocated justice for Ferguson to perform meetings in the Elks Club Hall. In a column, Winchell compared the events of not letting social justice groups use the Elks Club Hall and the recent vandalism of Rockville Centre Temple B'nai Sholom to relics of the American Nazi group Bund a decade before. In his column, he stated, "I have the deported American Nazi leader Fritz Kuhn's album which contained signatures of locals." Winchell openly challenged District Attorney Gehrig, saying, "Would you be interested in whose names are in the album?"[109]

The calls for justice also came from the neighboring town of Rockville Centre. In the early morning of June 8, Rockville Centre police received a call to 15 Wellington Place to bust an illegal gambling operation. When officers arrived, they discovered only one person at the residence, preacher William Dessaure, and no evidence of illegal gambling. Officer Arthur L'Hommedieu, a former boxer, claimed that he was attacked by Dessaure, which resulted in Dessaure being beaten by him and fellow officer Louis Wells with nightsticks. The beating resulted in stitches and extensive injuries to Dessaure. Dessaure was charged and arrested for assault on both officers. After the arrest, Dessaure claimed that when the officers got to Wellington Place, a verbal argument occurred between him and the officers. L'Hommedieu took his nightstick and struck him multiple times out of frustration in finding no illegal gambling.

Further damaging the creditability of L'Hommedieu was his rumored ties to gambling and loan shark operations outside of the Rockville Centre Police Department. Officer Wells countered following Dessaure's complaint, stating that the injuries happened when Dessaure went to the precinct after Dessaure tried reaching for their nightsticks.[110] The Ferguson family lawyer, Stanley Faulkner, quickly picked up the case to defend Dessaure, demanding a probe into the beating and further urging the state to probe the deaths of the Ferguson brothers. Lumping both the Ferguson brothers' murders and the beating of Dessaure together, Faulkner used the events to argue that police brutality in Nassau County needed to be investigated. By June 15, the clergy and the Ferguson justice groups were holding daily rallies in New York City and outside the state capitol in Albany. The city rallies for the Ferguson brothers gained more allies in the clergy. The protests and delegation to Governor Dewey's office argued that a state probe was needed for the Nassau County "whitewashed" investigations.[111]

After five months of protesting and counter-protesting, Governor Dewey agreed to a public state probe into the shooting deaths of Charles and Alphonso. Dewey was running for another term as governor against Democrat James

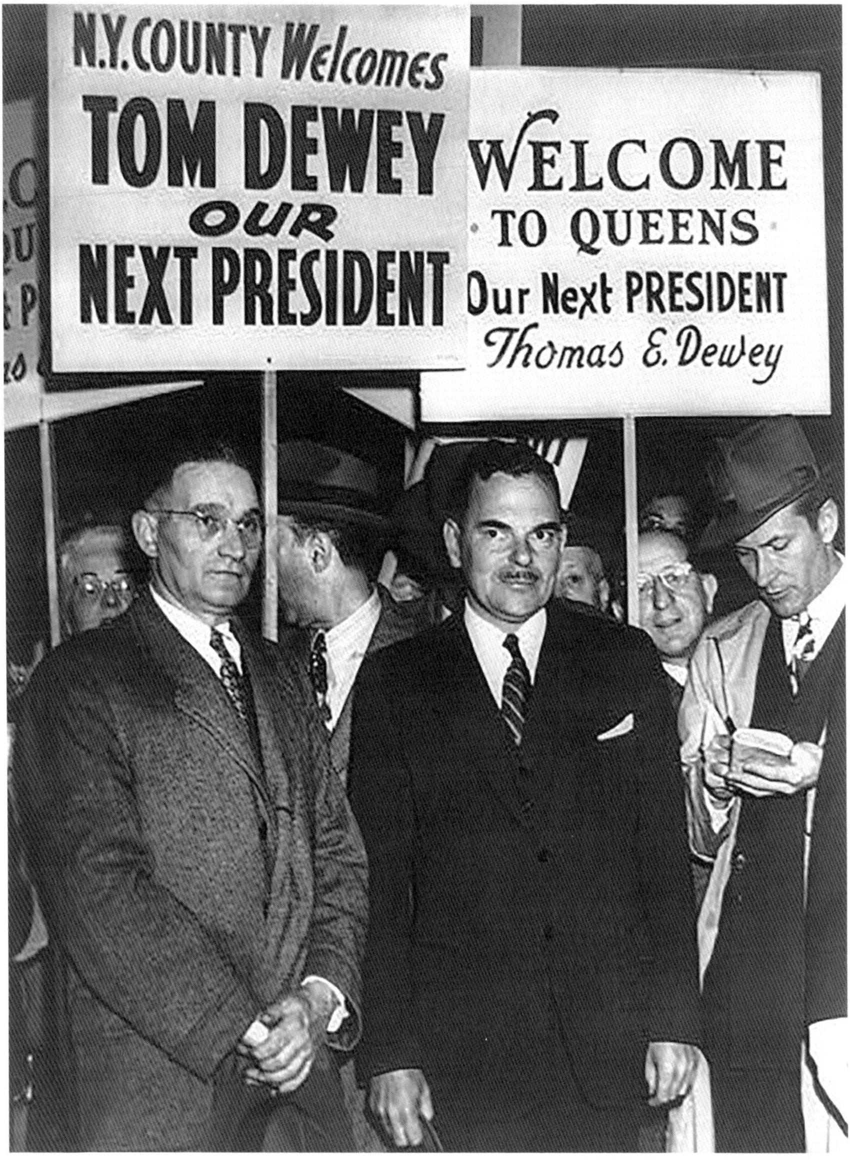

New York State Governor Thomas Dewey at a rally for his party's nomination for president. *Courtesy of the Library of Congress.*

Mead. While serving as a federal senator for New York, Mead proposed that the focus of the Senate following the close of World War II should be to declare war on poverty and discrimination. The centerpiece of Mead's political career was antipoverty and his stance against discrimination. Dewey, as a governor, wrote and passed one of the first state civil rights laws but wanted to enhance his civil rights record further, and the probe would have been an ideal political decision to achieve that goal. In response to Dewey agreeing to conduct a probe, James Gehrig wrote a letter to Dewey protesting his decision. Gehrig stated, "I am satisfied that justice was promptly and unqualifiedly served in this case; I regret that the proof has been covered by the rule of secrecy relating to Grand Jury proceedings. Organizations have interested themselves in injecting racial implications into the matter. I respectfully urge that the petition into a probe should be dismissed."[112]

Despite the request days earlier, on July 5, Dewey appointed Lawrence Greenbaum to lead the investigation. The investigation would have the authority to revisit all known evidence of the case, collect additional physical evidence, call multiple witnesses to a series of hearings and make recommendations to indict Officer Romeika for the shootings. Greenbaum was chairman of the New York State Board of Welfare and an active member of the NAACP. In addition to his position within the state and affiliation with the NAACP, Greenbaum had experience conducting civil rights investigations. Years prior, Greenbaum investigated discrimination against women of color in the Hudson Training School.[113] But more important than his credentials was the fact that he was from and lived in Mamaroneck and was appointed by Democratic Governor Herbert Lehman. Having a person not associated with Nassau County and selected by an opposing party/different administrations would have been an attempt to keep integrity in conducting the probe. Leaders within Dewey's party, such as Joseph Carlino, made their opinions public about the case, and his influence over the state Republican Party could hamper any probe. Once the probe was announced, the Nassau Conference of Human Rights appealed to Greenbaum to hold the hearings for the probe in Nassau. In response to the demand for objectivity, Greenbaum scheduled the hearings for New York City. In contrast to his correspondence with the governor, Gehrig affirmed to the reporters that he "urged the probe prior and hopes all information in the hands of the grand jury will be reviewed by the state and be brought out at a public investigation."[114] On the first public appearance related to the probe, Greenbaum affirmed that he was only seeking the facts and that it was not a witch hunt.[115] On the opening day of the probe and the scheduling of hearings, July 12, Dewey appointed Sol Gelb, the former assistant district attorney for New York City. Gelb's role was to gather the testimonies for the hearings and question the witnesses. The first week of state hearings was scheduled for July 15.

Chapter 10

STATE PROBE AND SECRET FEDERAL PROBE

In late February, the FBI was contacted to investigate the Ferguson shootings and suspected communist groups associated with the calls for justice. Assistant Attorney General Theron Caudle issued the original memo to the New York FBI office director. The probe cited denial of the Ferguson brothers' due process, secured in United States Code, Section 52, Title 18, but did not address any other alleged violations of the brothers' civil rights. This was mainly due to the lack of federal jurisdiction. In 1964, the passage of the Civil Rights Act made civil rights violations a part of federal jurisdiction. The investigation was assigned to Special Agent W.A. Johnson, who completed his report by April 3. The investigation was kept from the press, Governor Dewey's administration, and most of the public. But who requested the investigation, and why was the bureau keeping it from the media and most state officials within Dewey's administration?

The request for the investigation had to come from a federal official with connections to the local political parties of Nassau County. Democratic congressman Clayton Powell, involved with the citizen groups that demanded justice, could have requested the investigation, but he was a freshman congressman. He represented not Nassau County but parts of Upstate New York, Harlem, and the Bronx. If the investigation were public, Powell would have benefited from the push to get a federal agency involved. But the investigation was kept out of public knowledge, so discretion was requested. The person who ordered the federal probe was Republican First Congressional District congressman Leonard Hall. Hall represented a large portion of Nassau County, including Freeport. The Republican Party brokers for Long Island were Hall and Assemblyman Joseph Carlino. Within Hempstead, the person who held much of the power for the Republican Party and communicated with Hall was Carlino. When Carlino issued his statement in the press about the criminal records of the brothers and his stance on the case, he had direct or indirect communication with the FBI. Carlino and Republican district attorney James Gehrig shared findings in the case with each other. In addition to being a lifelong Republican, Gehrig was the county secretary of the Nassau Republicans, chairman of the Republican Law Committee, and a former president of the Hempstead Republican Club.[116] The FBI report further confirmed this connection to the local Republican Party, noting that the bureau had been communicating with Hall and Gehrig since February 26. While the FBI was conducting the probe, it investigated the Ferguson's family lawyer, Stanley Faulkner, and justice advocate and former East Harlem congressman Vito Marcantonio in a separate investigation. Faulkner and Marcantonio were under surveillance for links to communist groups, which later expanded to both men being investigated under a House Un-American Activities Committee probe. The first page of the report about the shooting notes, "It is believed from some of the literature and mass meetings held in New York City and Long Island that they are sponsored by Communist interests as means of creating race hatred on the part of the Negros."[117] The overall FBI probe investigated the shooting, and most of its concern centered on the suspected communist groups involved in the calls for justice. In the final memo on April 22, the FBI report recommended that "no need for any additional investigation into the shooting, and no criminal proceeding was warranted."

While the FBI's probe was conducted, the state justice department was not informed of the investigation or the findings. The entire completed report was not disclosed to Greenbaum when he was assigned to conduct his probe. Unlike the FBI investigation, the press publicly reported Greenbaum's probe throughout the hearings, which were open for the public to attend. Greenbaum's probe focused not on communist threats but on the events of February 5. Both reports would ultimately have contradictory findings.

The state hearings were scheduled in the Bar Association Building on 42 West Avenue and 44th Street in Manhattan. On the opening day of the hearing, Greenbaum explained that "this investigation is under section 62 of the state Executive Law of New York and is not a trial. Counsel Sol Gelb will conduct questioning, who would be happy to receive suggestions from any party regarding possible witnesses or evidence. But I reserve full power to decide whether such evidence is within the scope of the terms of my appointment."[118] On July 15, a dozen witnesses were scheduled to be called to a crowded hearing with more than one hundred spectators. While the witnesses were called to provide their accounts, Faulkner and his colleague from the Lawyers Guild, Milton Paulson, were not permitted to question witnesses. The other lawyer on the Ferguson family's side was the NAACP's Franklin Williams, who remained silent during the hearings, offering no objections. The only person allowed to question the witnesses was Gelb, who Faulkner objected over during the first day of the hearings. Additional witnesses who did not testify in the original grand jury hearing included Joseph Langdon, Joseph Johnson, and Francis Meaney, all bus drivers who claimed to have witnessed the brothers in the tea room. Langdon was the driver on the same bus as Madeline Moher. Moher was the original witness who stated that the brothers were not disorderly before entering the tea room. Langdon confirmed her account. Meaney and Johnson testified that they saw Charles Ferguson and restaurant manager Gus Cholakis exchanging epithets not far from the bay where they parked their buses. This eyewitness account contradicted George Couloras's and Gus Cholakis's testimony that Charles yelled at him, and Gus remained silent and noncombative. Another inconsistency was in the early testimony from Cholakis and his friend Couloras that they were alone in the restaurant with the brothers. Meaney claimed that he was in the restaurant during the argument. In his testimony, Meaney recalled, "Charles picked up some cocoa that I was drinking and threw it on the floor and said he was going to kill a couple of White men and might as well start with me."[119] Meaney's account was not confirmed by any of the witnesses originally called for the grand jury hearing and the state probe.

Testimony from Richard, Joseph, Crummell, and Romeika held the most significant sway. Richard was the first witness to be called on July 17:

> *Gelb: What do you recall of the day of the shooting, and what time did you arrive in Freeport?*
>
> *Richard: We arrived in Freeport around midnight, and we went to the Texas Rangers and had hamburgers and coffee for about 15 minutes or longer. And then we went to the Terminal Tea room.*
>
> *Gelb: How long did you know Gus Cholakis, the Terminal Tea room manager?*

Richard: I had known Gus for two years before enlisting in the service.

Gelb: How often before February 4th were you in there?

Richard: Not very often, nine or ten times.

Gelb: For what?

Richard: Coffee.

Gelb: On this evening that the four of you were in this lunchroom, what happened in there?

Richard: We ordered coffee, and Gus told us he didn't have any; he would give us tea or cocoa. So one of my brothers [Charles] *insisted on having coffee.*

Gelb: Which one?

Richard: Charlie.

Gelb: After you were told that he had no more coffee and offered tea, what did Gus and Charles say to one another?

Richard: I do not know. I was not paying attention, but it was rough in there. Charles tried going behind the counter at Gus, and Joseph told him to come out, and we were going to the park [Bennington Park].

Gelb: Did he go or refuse to go?

Richard: He came.

Gelb: Where did you go when you left the lunchroom?

Richard: After we got Charles out, we went to The Nest, stayed there for about 15 to 20 minutes, and walked back to the terminal to catch a bus home.

Gelb: Did you all walk together?

Richard: We walked in twos. Charles and Allie [Alphonso] *were walking ahead, and me and Joseph about 25 feet behind them. I noticed Charlie and Allie talking to the officer as we caught up.*

Gelb: Have you seen the officer before?

Richard: No, I had not….

Gelb: Then what happened?

Richard: As we caught up, the officer kicked Charlie in his groins, and we walked up there and asked what was going on. The officer reached for his gun, and at this time, we were standing around the officer. He then kicked Joey, pulled his gun, and told us to stand against the wall.

Gelb: Had there been talking between the officer?

Richard: I did not hear what they said before we got there.

Gelb: What did the officer do then?

Richard: After he reached for his gun, he told us to stand up against the coal office with our hands up; as the officer was standing towards the end of the building, Charlie and Allie were arguing amongst each other with their hand up and then started to argue with the officer as to why they were stopped. Not sure at this point if the officer used the phone to call for a wagon.

Gelb: Up against the coal building?

Richard: Yes, with our hands up.

Gelb: Take a look at this picture. On the left, do you see a little building? Is that the coal building?

Richard: Yes

Gelb: Did he state you were under arrest?

Richard: He said he is calling the wagon.... Yes.

Gelb: Did they refuse arrest?

Richard: No, but they wanted to find out why we were being arrested.

Gelb: Did the officer say why they were under arrest?

Richard: I believe the officer might have said why. He avoided the subject of the broken window. I believe he said Gus called the police.

Gelb: All right. Now the officer had you lined up and cursing back and forth; what happened then?

Richard: I heard a shot go off. Even at that, I was not paying attention to him. I heard a second shot go off but did not figure it was anything. I did not see Charles and Alphonso fall, and I did not see the officer fire the shots. I did notice the officer coming around the front of us after the first shot and before I heard the second shot. Joey said he was hit in the shoulder. I didn't believe him, and I walked over to see what was the matter; I thought he was kidding. The officer told me to get away from him and put our hands back up. Joey was standing with his shoulder down, and the officer kept telling him to put his hands up too. I did not see Charles or Alphonso at this time.

Gelb: Where was the officer standing?

Richard: He was sort of standing on an angle, and I couldn't see him; he was like this [Richard indicated]. *He could look down the line and see us. He was more or less facing Charlie on my left.*

Gelb: What happened next?

Richard: The officer called for a wagon on the police box/phone about 15–20 feet away. The wagon came within minutes, and we were told to get in. When the wagon came, I saw Charles and Alphonso—lying on the ground. Charles was by the corner of the building on the left, and I think Alphonso was next to him. I was then taken to the station and charged with disorderly conduct.

Gelb: The Freeport Police Court hearing record shows no district attorney present. Did you know that?

Richard: No.

Gelb: The Freeport minutes state the substance of the case was cursing.

Richard: I can't quite follow you.

Gelb: In other words, what were they getting at in this cursing?

Richard: I was not paying attention to the cursing. I was feeling good.

Gelb: How many drinks did you have that night?

Richard: I had about seven or eight beers and three or four wines.

Gelb: Did Charles consume the same amount?

Richard: Maybe the same.

Richard was excused from the stand, and the court had a short recess. After the recess, Gelb called Joseph Ferguson to testify:

Gelb: What happened while you were in the lunchroom?

Joseph: We went in there and asked for a cup of coffee. He said he didn't have any coffee that he would give us. There was coffee in the urn, and still said he didn't have anything. I saw it. He insisted he did not have any coffee and would give us tea or something else. So my brother [Charles] *called to his attention that coffee was in the urn.*

Gelb: What happened?

Joseph: Somehow, a row come up, and a few words passed back and forth. Charles called him a Greek son of a bitch, but he called him [Charles] *a son of a bitch. Charles started going to the back of the counter, and I grabbed him. We came out.*

Gelb: Did you pass the office of the coal company?

Joseph: That is right.

Gelb: What happened there?

Joseph: Well, my brother [Charles] *put his foot through the window, and we went down to The Nest.*

Gelb: What happened as you passed the coal company towards the bus terminal after leaving The Nest?

Joseph: We were 20 to 25 feet behind Charles and Alphonso when a police officer stepped out. The officer either stopped my brothers or something. I knew they were talking, but I could not hear them. The officer asked, "Did we go through there before" when we caught up. And someone said no. Then the officer pulled his gun and said we were under arrest, and Charles asked: "For what."

Gelb: And then what else happened?

Joseph: The officer told us to get against the wall and started calling us bastards and saying get over against the wall. The officer said, "You can't come down here and try to kill people." The officer then kicked Charles in the groins and me in the hip.

Gelb: Was Charles saying anything to the officer?

Joseph: He kept asking what we were under arrest for. Charles wanted to know what we were under arrest for, and the officer replied, threatening to kill somebody and "You can't come down here getting tough."

Gelb: What did Charles say?

Joseph: Charles called him a son of a bitch, and he called us bastards again. Charles said he might have a .45. Before that, Herman Crummell came up. Then as he walked up to the officer, he too was ordered against the wall. After Charles said he might have a .45, there was no more talking at this point. When he said I might have a.45, I turned towards him because I knew he did not have a gun.

Gelb: What happened?

Joseph: Charles leaned over, kind of slow as if he was falling forward. While falling, he had both hands up; he then started to drop his right hand by his hip. Like a man under the influence of drink, he fell, and one hand dropped like this [indicating].

Gelb: When you testified in front of the Grand Jury, do you remember saying that when Charles said he might have a .45, he "reached slowly down towards his pocket."

Joseph: It was the same thing as I said. His right hand slowly lowered to his hip.

Gelb: What did the officer do?

Joseph: The officer fired at the movement as Charles lowered his left hand....Before his hand reached hip level. Then the second shot right after. I did not see Charles drop. I saw Alphonso drop on my right side; I was two feet from Alphonso. I did not see Alphonso move before the second shot.

Gelb: How were you guys lined up?

Joseph: We were kind of standing in a zig-zag. Alphonso was sort of behind me on my left.

Gelb: Where was the officer standing?

Joseph: His back was facing the fence. [indicated from the picture].

Gelb: You were more or less on the side of the building that looks upon the bus terminal?

Joseph: That is right.

Gelb: After Charles dropped his hand and he fell, and Alphonse fell, what happened?

Joseph: The policeman changed his position and walked around with his back facing the tracks.

Gelb: Then what happened?

Joseph: The officer pulled out his handkerchief and started to mop his face. He did not say anything, and at this time, I realized I was shot. The patrol wagon came shortly after….

Gelb: Was your original testimony substantially to the same effect as the testimony you gave here?

Joseph: The best of my recollection.

Gelb: Did you tell the Navy officer any other statements?

Joseph: The condition I was. I was all confused. I guess it was about the best I could do at that time.

Joseph was dismissed from the stand, and Herman Crummell was next to be called to testify. His testimony contrasted sharply with his initial statements at the police station on February 5, his testimony at the Nassau County Grand Jury, and the various affidavits:

Gelb: What did you see when you arrived at the bus terminal in the early morning hours of February 5th?

Crummell: I saw the Ferguson boys and a cop in front of them, and they seemed to be swearing at one another. Hard language back in forth. Most of the cursing was coming from Charles. I stopped by to see the trouble, and the cop had me put my hands up and stand against the wall. I remember the officer saying, you are under arrest, and the Ferguson boys had words back and forth, and the cop said, "Keep your hands up and back up to the wall."

Gelb: Did Charles say anything about the arrest?

Crummell: No. Not at the present time. Then Charles said, you ain't going to arrest me and all that kind. Practically all of them were talking. I think.

Gelb: What was Alphonse doing at this time?

Crummell: I do not know. Alphonso was at the end.

Gelb: How were they lined up?

Crummell: Charles was on my left, Richard was on my right, and Alphonso was last.

Gelb: All right…start over again. The line started from one end of the building, is that right?

Crummell: Charles was standing on the edge of the corner. I tried to tell you this. I was next to Charles, Richard next to Joseph, and Alphonso.

Gelb: What happened then?

Crummell: He told us to put our hands up and back up to the wall. He had it out (the officer had his gun), and then Charles hollered; he had a .45 and dropped his hand. The first time the cop made him get his hands up. The second time he dropped his hands, the officer shot him.

Gelb: Was it the right hand he dropped?

Crummell: I guess so. The first time, he dropped it, and then the second time, he dropped his hand for his back pocket. Then the cop shot him.

Gelb: Did you see Charles fall?

Crummell: I looked at Charles. It looked like he was laying down, and I saw Allie was on the ground in front of my foot. Practically.

Gelb: Did you see Alphonso do anything?

Crummell: No, I did not exactly.

Gelb: How far in front of you was Alphonso shot?

Crummell: Ten feet, something like that. It happened so fast—the shots.

Gelb: You testified before the grand jury in Nassau County.

Crummell: Yes, I did.

Gelb: Do you remember being asked What did Alphonso do? And you answered, "Alphonso, the little one tried to rush the cop, and the cop shot him." Do you remember that answer?

Crummell: No. I do not remember that part.

Gelb: Do you remember this? When did he try to rush the cop? Your reply, "After Charles got shot."

Crummell: I do not remember everything. He may have because otherwise—he is down there by me. He had to get in the line somehow—like he was right down by us in the front.

Gelb: When he was shot, where was he?

Crummell: Laying right down on the ground by me?

Gelb: Charles was laying in front of you too?

Crummell: Yes.

Gelb: Alphonso was to his right?

Crummell: Yes, sir.

Gelb: Crossways?

Crummell: Yes.

Gelb: Did Alphonso rush the cop or not?

Crummell: I really do not remember.

Gelb: You remember saying Alphonse ran out of line?

Crummell: Yes.

Gelb: Where did he go?

Crummell: He started towards his brothers. No, I mean Joe was the first one to start out of the line.

Gelb: Joe, what?

Crummell: Joe started to go out of the line, and Alphonso—I do not know it happened so quickly.

Gelb: You swore before a grand jury that Alphonso rushed the cop, did you not?

Crummell: That's right.

Gelb: You do not know whether he rushed the cop or not?

Crummell: No.

Gelb: You had a statement taken at the police station, questioned by the district attorney, appeared before a grand jury, testified in the police court, testified in front of the mayor, and gave additional affidavits. Is that right?

Crummell: Yes.

Gelb: In an affidavit on April 5th, you said: "I looked back at the cop and then saw him stretch his arm out, take aim and fire." The affidavit reads, "up to that time, the cop's arm was in a bent position resting against his body, but at the time he took the first shot, he stretched his arm out, aimed, and fired. He was about eight to ten feet away from us." This is in the affidavit you signed. Did he or did he not take aim and fire?

Crummell: I do not know whether he took aim, but I know he fired—I DON'T KNOW….

Gelb: Did anyone suggest to you what to say or threaten you?

Crummell: No.

Later in the hearing, Arnold Johnson, a lawyer assisting from the Lawyers Guild, asked the court to note the appearance of Crummell after he left the police station in the early morning hours of February 5. Johnson stated, "The young man had lacerations on his face following his visit to the police station." Johnson also noted that Crummell's "statement was incoherent." Crummell was then dismissed from the stand.

The following person to testify was Joseph Romeika. Like with Crummell and Joseph's testimonies, Romeika's original grand jury testimony was inconsistent with the statements given during the Greenbaum probe. Romeika claimed that all the brothers came at him during the probe threateningly:

Gelb: After Gus reported to you that he was threatened and the window was broken by one of the Ferguson brothers, what happened next?

Romeika: I saw the four colored men approaching me. When they approached me, they said, "You fucking cop, we are not afraid of you." I asked what the problem was, and they continued to use abusive language. I told them to shut up, and they came at me. I kicked one and drew my revolver, and I kicked one and shoved the other.

Gelb: What do you mean the four came at you?

Romeika: They came at me with their fists up. All of them.

Gelb: Then what happened?

Romeika: I told them they were under arrest and marched them to box 14 near the terminal, made a call for a wagon, and marched them back to the coal company wall. Crummell then came along and asked what the trouble was. I had him go against the wall. Charles then said I would kill you, and next time you walk down Bennington Park—I will kill you. Charles then said he had a .45. I said, keep your hands up. Charles was standing on my left, and his hand went into his back pocket, and I shot him. Alphonso then jumped at me on my left, and I shot him—within a second. I held and fired the gun at hip level.

Gelb: You did not raise your hand and shoot.

Romeika: I did not raise my hand at all.

Gelb: How tall are you?

Romeika: Six feet one inch.

Gelb: Between the first and second shots, according to your description, just a second elapsed, or not even a second?

Romeika: About a second, not even a second.

Gelb: What happened after the shooting?

Romeika: Sergeant Wulff came down with the wagon, and the brothers said, "You won't get away with this," and things like that. I charged Richard and Joseph for disturbing the peace.

Gelb: One was shot and wounded?

Romeika: Yes, Joseph had a shoulder wound. I fired two bullets, but I didn't know whether one was hit; laying on the ground, I thought one of them was playing phony.

Gelb: You thought one was pretending?

Romeika: That is right.

Gelb: Did you ever shoot a man while on duty or at that time?

Romeika: No, sir. Sergeant Wulff arrived, and he assisted me, and being that Charles mentioned something about a.45, I thought that would likely be that .45 Gus Cholakis mentioned in the terminal. When I asked Gus if he knew these men, he said they were the same four that molested him.

Gelb: Did you find any .45?

Romeika: He had no gun.

Gelb: You said you did not raise your arm above the hip level when you shot Charles?

Romeika: No, sir. I did not raise my arm.

Gelb: Have you heard the medical examiner testify that the bullet went downward?

Romeika: Charles reached for his pocket, bent over like that [indicating], *reaching for his back pocket, and Alphonso came from my left.*

Gelb: You testified before the police court—I am reading from one answer here—"Mr. Gus Cholakis advised me that four men entered the Terminal Tea Room and threatened to kill him." Did you at any time in police court mention that Gus told you Charles had a .45?

Romeika: I don't remember whether I did or not.

Gelb: Your testimony covers two pages, and it is not there. Are you sure that is what Gus told you?

Romeika: I am positive.

Gelb: You did not mention that these four men had a .45. Do you testify now that Gus did tell you that?

Romeika: Yes, he did, he did. He said one of them claimed he had a .45—threatened him with a .45 in his pocket.

Gelb: You stated to the district attorney [Gelb reads the statement following the shooting] *you did not mention Gus telling you he was threatened with a .45.*

Following the testimonies of Richard and Joseph Ferguson, Crummell, and Romeika, more questions were raised than answers. Joseph admitted that his initial statements of the event varied due to his physical condition and confusion. Crummell's testimony changed from his initial claim that he saw Alphonso rushing the cop to never seeing Alphonso rush or move toward the officer. Crummell could not keep the story straight from where the brothers were lined up and what happened during the second shot. Romeika's story changed as to Gus's original complaint about whether he was threatened with a .45 or not.

Most of the questions during the state probe came from the medical examiner's report. The report, examined by Greenbaum, detailed that Charles's body revealed internal injuries from the kick. Charles's urethra was punctured and hemorrhaging. When Curphey testified, he was asked if the hemorrhaging of the urethra could be a result of a kick to the groin. Curphey replied yes. The other findings were that Charles and Alphonso were not legally drunk. The toxicologist, Dr. A.W. Freireich, working with the chief medical examiner of Nassau County, found alcohol present in the brain of Charles to be 0.2 percent and alcohol levels in Alphonso's brain to be 0.058 percent.[120] The level of alcohol in the brain needed to determine if someone was intoxicated at the time was 0.25 percent. This level of alcohol toxicity was the standard set in the *American Journal of Surgery* by Dr. Alexander Getter in 1935.

Charles's full autopsy report reflected that a bullet went into the left clavicle by the sternal joint and exited by the left intracapsular space (shoulder bone). The measurement used in the autopsy was an entry of fifty-five inches from the heel and an exit of fifty-one inches from the heel. The bullet entering the clavicle sternal area ripped into the aorta through where it joins the arch.[121] As a result of the hemorrhaging, the chest was filled with three pints of blood[122] (on average, a person has ten pints of blood; hemorrhaging 40 percent of the blood results in death). The total measurement of entry to exit was four inches. Charles had to be hunching over, and the officer fired the bullet at the level of Charles's head in a downward direction. These findings contradict the officer's claim that he fired the gun at waist level. Based on the entry and exit of the bullet and Joseph's testimony in front of the Greenbaum commission, Charles was falling forward as he was shot but could have had his left toe dragging on the pavement. His left shoe, by the toe, had scuffing, as noted in the full autopsy report. Other indications that Charles could have slipped are found in the sand on the left side of his face and his wearing brown Oxford shoes. The temperature was below freezing during the early morning hours of February 5. Freeport Public Works sanded the sidewalk and roadways where ice patches were most likely to form. Charles could have slipped in combination with the potential ice patches and the Oxford shoes with leather soles, which provided no grip.

Another detail to note was that Charles's height was five feet, eight inches, and he weighed 180 pounds. According to his draft card, Officer Romeika was six feet and 180 pounds. The height of both men also conflicts with Romeika's claim that Charles's hands were at his hips when shot. The direction of the bullet entry and exit is inconsistent with his hands at hip level.

Alphonso was killed by a bullet exiting Joseph's shoulder and going into his forehead above his right eye. Alphonso was five feet, two inches, and Joseph was five feet, ten inches. The height difference means Alphonso would be at or near shoulder level with Joseph by standing with a slight slouch. The bullet wound in Alphonso's head was shaped like a key. During the Greenbaum Commission, Curphey was asked about the key-shaped entry wound. Curphey replied, "It indicates the bullet did not come straight but probably tumbled in flight before entering Alphonso's head."[123] The bullet entered the left frontal lobe in a slightly downward trend, and the .38 round was recovered between the two halves of the brain. The second shot reflects no evidence that Alphonso tried attacking the officer since Alphonso had to be behind Joseph and was twenty-five feet away from the officer at the time of the shooting.

Overall, the state probe predetermination was that the officer had the brothers under arrest for several minutes. At this point, he could have determined if any of them had a gun. This predetermination was noted on the final day of the state probe.

On July 23, the third day into the hearings, citizen groups requested Greenbaum to detail the race relations in Freeport and Nassau County in the report to describe a more in-depth background into the civil rights challenges. Other additional requests came from a spectator named Dr. Ruth Foster, who asked Greenbaum to have Romeika recalled to the stand to testify on the inconsistencies of his statements. Foster noted that Romeika's statement that he was in front of the brothers and one of them was charging at him conflicted with the medical examiner's autopsy. Greenbaum, in response, said, "I have your letter which indicates your conclusion." Faulkner and Dorothy Langston protested that the probe did not further detail Gehrig's handling of the case and wanted more questions relating to the grand jury. Langston also requested the minutes of the grand jury be made public. When Greenbaum refused, Langston declared the case was "whitewashed" and stated, "I do not want anything to do with a hearing that is only interested in protecting the administration of Gehrig and not the truth." After Langston's speech, spectators shouted at Greenbaum, "You are guilty of the blood of the brothers," and, "This is not a democracy." Greenbaum, in response, told Langston and the spectators, "Kindly make your speeches in the hall." Langston then led half the spectators to protest the hearing in a walkout. In a *Newsday* interview, Langston told reporters that "not allowing the grand jury minutes to be public, limiting questioning of Gehrig and not allowing the Ferguson family attorney to question the witnesses reflect the governor never had the intentions of acting against a fellow Republican."[124]

Later in the day, Gehrig was called in to testify on his handling of the case. Gehrig was asked if he had asked a female witness whether she was a CIO union member in front of the grand jury. Gehrig responded, "Yes, I did ask the witnesses if they were union members because the Communist Party was agitating Freeport." Following Gehrig's response, attention was focused on his statement to the press: "If this were a white person shot by a white officer or a negro shot by a negro officer, there would be no fuss…or public agitation; on any matter."[125] Lawyers representing the Lawyers Guild requested Gelb to ask if that statement was before or after preparation for the grand jury hearing. Gehrig stated that it was before he prepared for the hearing. Greenbaum asked, "Did you assume that the grand jury read the papers and read what you stated"? Gehrig said, in reply to Greenbaum, "I do not know. I did not ask the grand jury." Another question from Gelb was why Romeika did not get suspended following the shooting. Gehrig responded that he spoke to Freeport Police Chief Elar about suspending Romeika. Gehrig told Elar that suspension of any officer was his jurisdiction and is routine if charges are filed. Gehrig further elaborated that Elar said to him that he would not suspend Romeika but instead put him on desk duty. In the final part of the series of questions, Gehrig was asked about his jury selection and why there were no non-white jurors. In response, Gehrig said that he was made aware of communist groups trying to influence communities of color by claiming, "Police shooting victims were people of color."

At the close of the third day of hearings, Greenbaum affirmed that this was the final hearing and that the results and recommendations would be announced in the coming weeks. After the walkout and the announced conclusion of the hearings, seventeen social justice groups—including the NAACP, American Jewish Congress, Socialist Workers Party, and American Veterans Committee—sent a joint telegram to Governor Dewey. The telegram stated, "The investigation is a fraud and can only follow the prejudiced path of the Nassau County Grand Jury. We demand that you supersede District Attorney Gehrig. No other action will be acceptable to the undersigned organizations."[126]

The first person called on the final day of hearings was Stanley Faulkner. While on the stand, Faulkner detailed his introduction to the case and interactions with the family, Gehrig, and the grand jury hearing. In closing,

Faulkner asked to read from a prepared statement, which Greenbaum permitted. Faulkner read:

> *Brute force was used in Germany and other European countries during the last war. This is something that these boys coming back from service did not expect to have encountered. Why do these similar situations arise from time to time? A certain barrier seems to exist among minority groups all the time. When this police officer encountered these negroes, he saw the danger coming. For example, the officer would have seen an Italian as an iceman or a Greek as a restaurant owner, but as a negro, he saw the danger. Therefore when a negro commits the crime of using profanity, it comes with a severer punishment, unlike a white person. These barriers made the cop fear his life once he saw the four negros. If nothing else comes out of the case, maybe there will be a change in these conditions.*

On August 2, 1946, the probe announced its findings. In a statement to the press, Greenbaum announced:

> *The Grand Jury's failure to indict Romeika can not be attributed to the district attorney in any way. The evidence the jury had concluded was that the officer had shot as he did in the performance of his duty. There is no evidence to establish that the officer, who thought his life was in danger, would have acted in any different manner had the four men before him been white and not colored. But, there is evidence of racial tensions following the death of the Ferguson brothers, which has no bearing on the conduct of Romeika. In my opinion, there is no case involving any violation of civil rights, nor is it an outcome of any discrimination on the part of the district attorney.*[127]

Greenbaum further explained that the "racial tensions in the community of Freeport cannot be remedied through any legal proceedings." The following day, Governor Dewey announced that the probe was officially closed. The response to the probe came with much criticism. A lawyer for the Congress of Industrial Organizations stated, "Whitewashed and a model report for Governor Talmadge and his Georgia lynching" (this statement referred to Georgia Governor Talmadge, who was believed to have sanctioned the lynching of four Black men in 1946).

But the state probe findings differed from those in the FBI report. In the latter, the primary difference in the autopsy part of the probe was not the wounds or alcohol levels but rather what determined intoxication.

The FBI determined intoxication at 0.15 percent BAC. At the time of his death, Charles was 0.20 percent, which was 0.05 percent above the FBI's standard. At the level of .058 percent, Alphonso was not intoxicated when he was shot. In contrast to the FBI report, Dr. Curphey, the medical examiner for Nassau County, reported that Alphonso, seven hours after ingestion, would have shown inconclusive results. The FBI's report does not address the inconsistency that the officer fired his gun waist-high despite the medical examiner concluding that the bullet had been fired downward. The report also does not dispute whether Alphonso tried to attack the officer but further affirms the direction of the bullet from Joseph's shoulder into Alphonso's forehead. The report does not question whether the shooting of Alphonso was justified but restates Romeika's statement as justification. In the state probe, the shooting of Alphonso was deemed avoidable and had no justification. The probe argued, "It appears to be no justification for firing a second shot. Alphonso…suffered death from the bullet that passed through the shoulder of Joseph and therefore not in such proximity to the officer as to bear any evidence of an attack."[128]

The district attorney's handling of the grand jury hearings was detailed in the state probe but left out in the FBI investigation. District Attorney Gehrig cited that he was hesitant to call witnesses requested by Ferguson family attorney Stanley Faulkner because of potential communist connections. A letter to the National Lawyers Guild from Gehrig's office stated, "Various organizations of the Communist Party or American Labor Party have presented names of witnesses who are being placed before the grand jury." During the hearing, Gehrig questioned the credibility of witnesses because of their memberships in labor unions. The state probe concluded that "no witnesses were turned over for examination or otherwise by any communist affiliated groups or groups Faulkner represented."

After the probe's conclusion, local newspaper editor George W. Goeller from the *Freeport Leader* requested a copy of the report to print in full. In a letter to Dewey, Goeller stated, "I lived in Freeport for 27 years, and it was not until some outsiders butted in that I discovered I was living in an intolerant community."[129] In response to the letter, Dewey's office sent a copy of Greenbaum's investigation results. But despite this, the probe was never published in the *Freeport Leader*. From the start of the Ferguson case to the end of the state probe, the *Leader* featured no more than a column's worth of space in a few papers covering the developments in the case. *Newsday*, the *New York Times*, and the *Brooklyn Daily Eagle* featured the most detailed coverage of the case. The *Freeport Leader*'s lack of coverage could have been due to the mayor's office or the local chamber of commerce, which wanted to put the event behind them and not further stigmatize the village.

Many groups had more questions than answers, and this mobilized one final push to reopen the Ferguson shooting case. Freeport's Northeast Civic Association, which supported Romeika and the Freeport Police Department throughout the probe, wrote a letter to Dewey commending the conclusion of the investigation. As stated in the letter, "The inquiry is closed by all governmental agencies, and this will end all the further agitation [against the community of Freeport]." After the results, many groups pushing for the state probe dropped their calls for justice. The American of Foreign War Post No. 25, Admiral Farragut Garrison Post, was the oldest and most prominent veteran post. The Garrison Post led the demand for a state probe months prior. In a letter to Dewey, post leader John Smith thanked him for conducting the probe and "disclosing the very true findings."

Dewey was up for reelection, and Democrat challenger James Mead promised to reopen the state probe once elected. Mead's campaign promises enabled Dorothy Langston to build on the New York Committee for Justice in Freeport. Letter campaigns were organized with the union leadership to pressure Dewey's administration. Labor unions that participated in the letter-writing campaigns or solidarity protests included United Auto Workers Ford Local 952 in Michigan; United Auto and Aircraft Workers of America of Michigan; Building Service Union Local 202 in Spokane, Washington; United Electrical & Radio Machine Workers of America in Philadelphia, Pennsylvania; CIO Council of Los Angeles; Leather Workers Union Local 34 of Hoboken, New Jersey; Endicott Leather Workers Union; United Metal Workers of America of Chicago, Illinois; Fur Dressers and Dyers Union of New York City; National Federation of Post Office Clerks; Marine Communications Local 2; Utility Workers Union of Los Angeles; Oil Workers International; Long Shoreman Unions of New Jersey/California; Garment Workers Union of New York City; and Tri-City Newspaper Guild Local 34 of New York. Labor demonstrations across northeastern cities inspired universities such as the University of Buffalo to hold a mass demonstration of students and faculty to protest the Freeport killings.

Following the overwhelming calls for justice, fellowship groups took hold and pushed the second wave of organizing, which was more widespread than what had taken place before the state probe. The most vocal religious groups included multiple AME churches across New York, First Congregational church congregations, Methodist churches stretching as far as South Dakota,

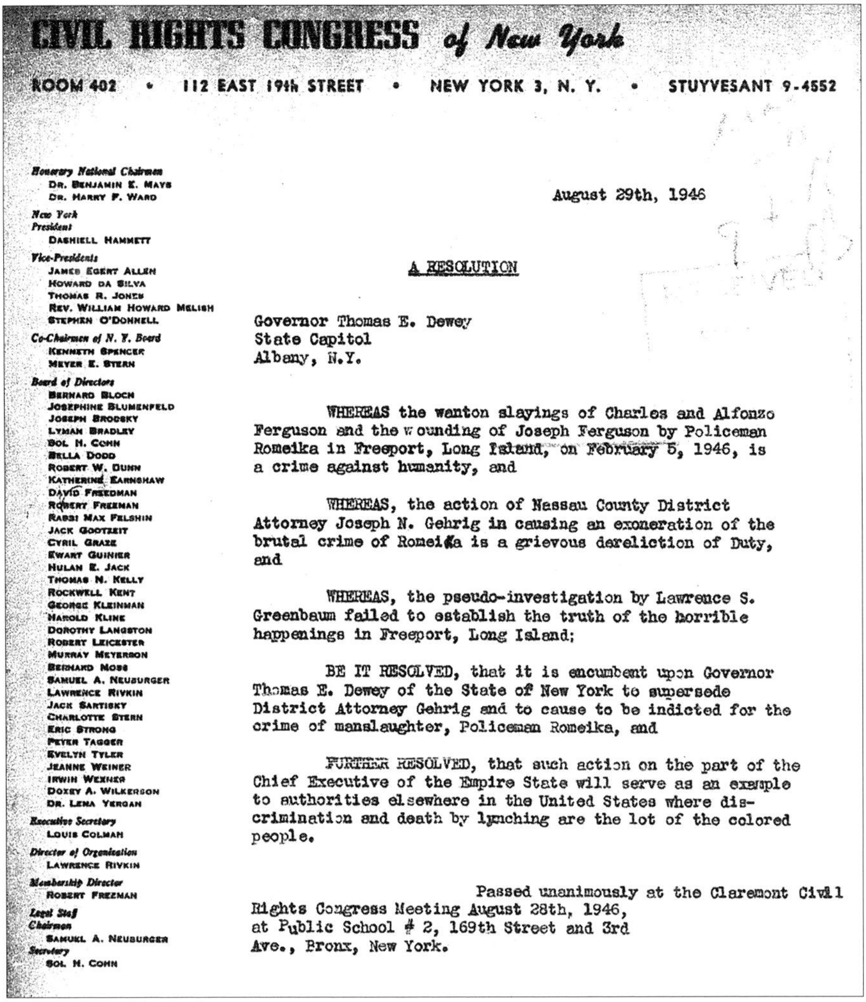

CIVIL RIGHTS CONGRESS *of New York*

ROOM 402 • 112 EAST 19th STREET • NEW YORK 3, N. Y. • STUYVESANT 9-4552

Honorary National Chairmen
Dr. Benjamin E. Mays
Dr. Harry F. Ward
New York
President
Dashiell Hammett
Vice-Presidents
James Egert Allen
Howard da Silva
Thomas R. Jones
Rev. William Howard Melish
Stephen O'Donnell
Co-Chairmen of N. Y. Board
Kenneth Spencer
Meyer E. Stern
Board of Directors
Bernard Bloch
Josephine Blumenfeld
Joseph Brodsky
Lyman Bradley
Sol H. Cohn
Bella Dodd
Robert W. Dunn
Katherine Earnshaw
David Freedman
Robert Freeman
Rabbi Max Felshin
Jack Gootzeit
Cyril Graze
Ewart Guinier
Hulan E. Jack
Thomas N. Kelly
Rockwell Kent
George Kleinman
Harold Kline
Dorothy Langston
Robert Leicester
Murray Meyerson
Bernard Moss
Samuel A. Neuburger
Lawrence Rivkin
Jack Sartisky
Charlotte Stern
Eric Strong
Peter Tagger
Evelyn Tyler
Jeanne Weiner
Irwin Wexner
Doxey A. Wilkerson
Dr. Lena Yergan
Executive Secretary
Louis Colman
Director of Organization
Lawrence Rivkin
Membership Director
Robert Freeman
Legal Staff
Chairman
Samuel A. Neuburger
Secretary
Sol H. Cohn

August 29th, 1946

A RESOLUTION

Governor Thomas E. Dewey
State Capitol
Albany, N.Y.

WHEREAS the wanton slayings of Charles and Alfonzo Ferguson and the wounding of Joseph Ferguson by Policeman Romeika in Freeport, Long Island, on February 5, 1946, is a crime against humanity, and

WHEREAS, the action of Nassau County District Attorney Joseph N. Gehrig in causing an exoneration of the brutal crime of Romeika is a grievous dereliction of Duty, and

WHEREAS, the pseudo-investigation by Lawrence S. Greenbaum failed to establish the truth of the horrible happenings in Freeport, Long Island;

BE IT RESOLVED, that it is encumbent upon Governor Thomas E. Dewey of the State of New York to supersede District Attorney Gehrig and to cause to be indicted for the crime of manslaughter, Policeman Romeika, and

FURTHER RESOLVED, that such action on the part of the Chief Executive of the Empire State will serve as an example to authorities elsewhere in the United States where discrimination and death by lynching are the lot of the colored people.

Passed unanimously at the Claremont Civil Rights Congress Meeting August 28th, 1946, at Public School # 2, 169th Street and 3rd Ave., Bronx, New York.

A formal petition to Governor Thomas Dewey from the Civil Rights Congress of New York, disputing the findings of the state probe. The petition demanded that Officer Romeika be indicted on manslaughter charges. *Courtesy of the University of Rochester's Thomas Dewey Archives.*

Pentecostal churches throughout the Northeast, Jewish fellowship groups in New York City, and Christian Fellowship Houses. A letter to Dewey from Jeannette Jamison of the Fellowship House in Reading, Pennsylvania, noted:

> *This event* [the shooting of the Ferguson brothers] *is the sort of thing that happened in Germany that aroused our people and people in other lands to fight Nazism in the frightful war. You were an active opponent of*

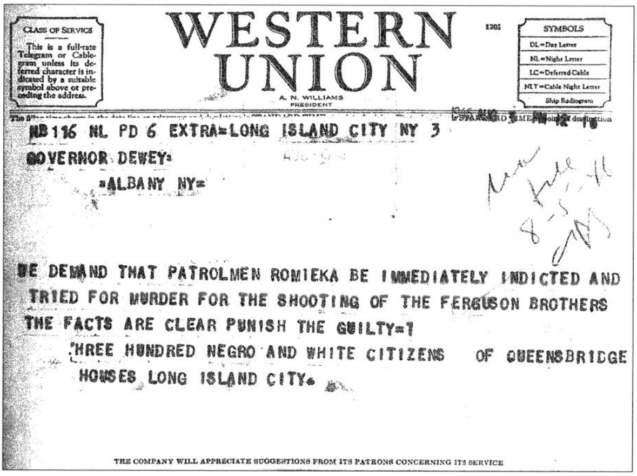

CLASS OF SERVICE
This is a full-rate Telegram or Cablegram unless its deferred character is indicated by a suitable symbol above or preceding the address.

WESTERN UNION

A. N. WILLIAMS
PRESIDENT

SYMBOLS
DL=Day Letter
NL=Night Letter
LC=Deferred Cable
NLT=Cable Night Letter
Ship Radiogram

NB116 NL PD 6 EXTRA=LONG ISLAND CITY NY 3
GOVERNOR DEWEY=
=ALBANY NY=

WE DEMAND THAT PATROLMEN ROMIEKA BE IMMEDIATELY INDICTED AND TRIED FOR MURDER FOR THE SHOOTING OF THE FERGUSON BROTHERS THE FACTS ARE CLEAR PUNISH THE GUILTY=?
THREE HUNDRED NEGRO AND WHITE CITIZENS OF QUEENSBRIDGE HOUSES LONG ISLAND CITY.

THE COMPANY WILL APPRECIATE SUGGESTIONS FROM ITS PATRONS CONCERNING ITS SERVICE

One of the hundreds of telegrams sent to Governor Dewey's office to protest the state probe findings. The telegram here is from a collective group of residents from the Queensbridge Houses in Queens, New York. *Courtesy of the University of Rochester's Thomas Dewey Archives.*

> *Nazi Germany, were you not? It is more than obvious that this event is un-American and un-Christian. In pictures, officer Romeika resembles a Nazi youth. At least discharge this officer from police service in the name of your self-respect.*

Echoing these sentiments were the town hall meetings of the AME church of Flushing, which attracted more than five hundred people to an anti-lynching and justice in Freeport rally. Speakers at the rally requested the attendees, their extended family, and friends to write to Dewey and demand justice for the Ferguson brothers. More than three hundred people crowded into the streets at 134th Street and Lenox Avenue and demanded that District Attorney Gehrig be suspended, Romeika charged with murder, and all estimated 1,100 Klan members within the state of New York have their names made public. But like all other letters and demonstrations demanding justice, Dewey's office sent them a letter of acknowledgment and a copy of the Greenbaum report. The transparency of sharing the report would change following advice from his legal counsel during Dewey's reelection.

As widespread as it was, the second wave of activism did not lead to justice or the removal of Romeika from the police force. Despite the questions about the shootings, changing of eyewitness testimonies, and the communist hysteria surrounding the case (which was argued by Gehrig both in the grand jury and state probe), the probe failed to bring about any justice for Alphonso and Charles Ferguson. While Dewey won reelection, Faulkner attempted to make the William Dessaure case of police brutality the main headline. Months earlier, charged for assaulting Rockville Centre police officers despite being beaten by at least two officers at the precinct,

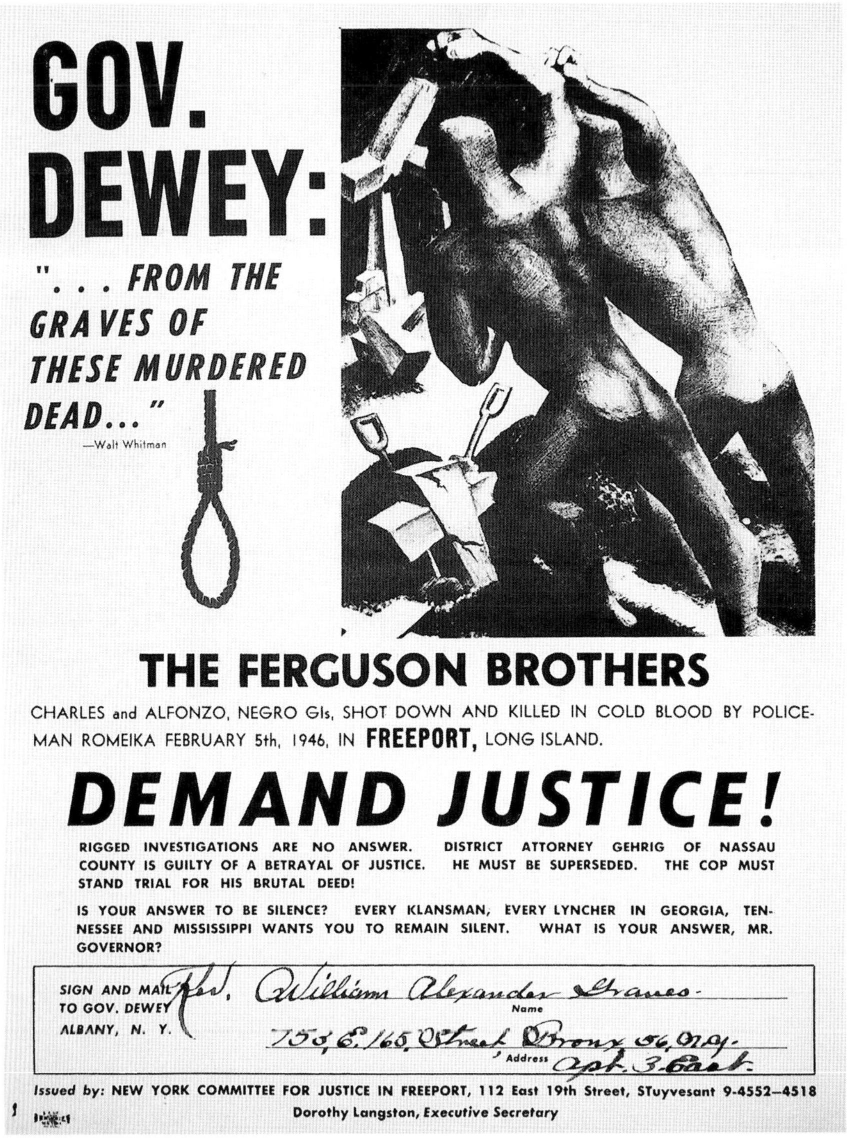

An organized letter campaign petition. The Dewey Archives has thousands of these petitions filed. *Courtesy of the University of Rochester's Thomas Dewey Archives.*

Dessaure faced up to three years in jail. The attention to his case worked to further activists' calls for a state probe in the Ferguson murders, claiming that structural racism in the local police force was reinforcing police brutality within the Black community. By May 1947, Dessaure had been convicted of second-degree assault by an all-white jury and sentenced to one and a half to three years in prison. An appeal was filed because no person of color served on the jury or any county trial in the previous ten years. The argument was based on the Sixth Amendment right to have a jury of your peers and the Fourteenth Amendment's equal protection under the law. Despite the legal arguments, the state court of appeals would not hear the case and upheld the lower court's decision. It would take the federal Supreme Court's ruling in *Batson v. Kentucky* (1986) to institute a ban on racial bias in jury selection.

Despite the failure to bring charges against Romeika for the Ferguson brothers' deaths, the most significant effect of the shooting was that it set in motion a groundswell desire for change throughout the nation. At the same time, it helped create a movement for civil rights due to the publicity and grass-roots organizing. Although a foundation for civil rights activism was formed from these events, Freeport and the surrounding communities would soon see regression in civil rights gains.

Chapter 11

AFTERMATH AND THE CIVIL RIGHTS STRUGGLES THAT FOLLOW

The New York State probe played out in the press in great detail every day. The testimony of Joseph Ferguson helped confirm the officer's claim that Charles stated he had a .45, despite no gun being recovered from any of the Ferguson brothers. Charles's alleged statement of having a .45 was no justification for the shooting but a precursor to the escalation of the events. Parallel to the events in Freeport and the state probe, Sergeant Isaac Woodard was recovering from his near-death beating at the hands of South Carolina police. As a result of the assault, Woodard was blinded for life. Similar to Charles, Woodard was brutalized by police while in his uniform. The flurry of civil rights activism reached out to world-renowned actors and musicians and did not lose momentum in shifting to Woodard. The cries of justice for Charles and Alphonso did not become silent; instead, they turned to also demand justice for Woodard and the need for a federal civil rights law.

On July 28, 1946, Orson Welles spoke the words that became a battle cry for justice on his ABC radio-based commentary:

> *The affidavit* [Isaac Woodard's eyewitness account] *seems to become a permanent part of my mental luggage. The boy* [Isaac Woodard] *saw him while he could still see. Still, of course, he had no way of knowing what particular policeman it was who brought the justice of Dachau and Oswiecim to Aiken, South Carolina. He was just another white man with a stick who wanted to teach a Negro boy*

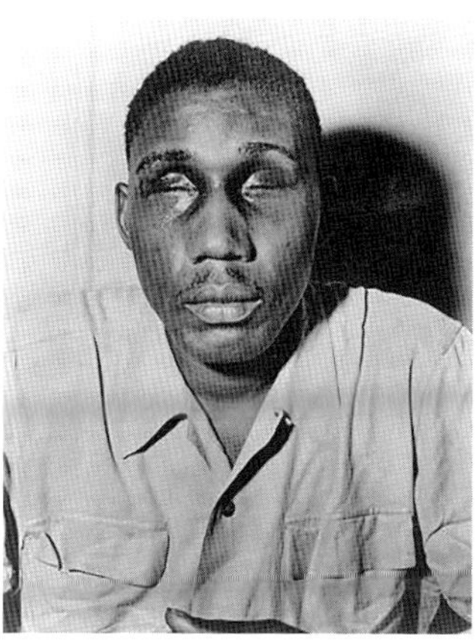

Sergeant Isaac Woodard recovered from his near-death beating at the hands of South Carolina police, although he was blinded for life. *Courtesy of the Library of Congress.*

> *a lesson—to show a Negro boy where he belonged: In the darkness. Till we know more about him, for just now we'll call the policeman Officer X. He might be listening to this...I hope so. Officer X, I am talking to you. The accumulated ignorance of the feudal south. And with a peculiar briefing, they called Cain for another day of the devil's work. While Abel slept, wash your hands, Officer X. Wash them well. Scrub and scour; you won't blot out the blood of a blinded war veteran. Nor yet the color of your skin. Your own skin. You'll never, never change it. Wash your hands, Officer X. Wash a lifetime; you'll never wash away that leprous lack of pigment—the guilty pallor of the white man. We invite you to luxuriate in secrecy. It will be brief. Go on, suckle your anonymous moment while it lasts. You're going to be uncovered. We will blast out your name! We'll give the world your given name; it's going to rise out of the filthy deep like the dead thing it is. We're going to make it public with the public scandal you dictated but failed to sign. Nothing in this world is free. The free air costs you the life-consuming effort of breath. Freedom itself is priced at the rate of the citizenship it earns and holds. What does it cost to be a Negro? In Aiken, South Carolina, it costs a man his eyes. What does it cost to wear over your skeleton a pinkish tint officially described as "white"? In Aiken, South Carolina, it cost a man his soul. Officer X may languish in jail. It's unlikely, but it isn't possible he'll serve as long a term as a Negro stealing bread. But Officer X will never pay for the two eyes he beat out of the soldier's head.*[130]

Welles's rallying call followed Woody Guthrie's song "The Blinding of Isaac Woodard," performed in a packed Lewisohn Stadium at City College of New York. The NAACP concert/fundraiser raised money and awareness, with the audience hanging on to every detail of Woodard's blinding through Guthrie's lyrics. Nat King Cole performing in front of sold-out audiences highlighted the Woodard blinding to audience members following his shows, which furthered calls for justice. Other artists and celebrities who participated in or organized fundraisers for the Ferguson brothers also actively supported justice for Woodard. The swiftness of the mobilization for Woodard soon overshadowed the Ferguson brothers' deaths. By the end of the summer, President Harry Truman had appointed a civil rights commission to investigate the blinding of Woodard. The response initiated a split in the Democrat Party between the Southern Democrats, Dixiecrats, and the moderate party members. Moderates began to mobilize around ideas that would later become the Civil Rights Act.

On September 26, the justice department opened a case and filed criminal charges against Sheriff Lynwood Shull. The Woodard case would be the first time a civil rights statute was used in a prosecution since Reconstruction.[131] But Sheriff Lynwood Shull was acquitted by an all-white jury. Despite this case's acquittal, the federal government set the example that it would intervene in civil rights violations. This grass-roots organization and rallying of moderate politicians would become the cornerstone of pushing for a federal civil rights law. The unintended consequence of the Woodard case included civil rights struggles, and fights were redirected from the North to the South. Northern civil rights demands were overshadowed, and reforms stalled. Following the acquittal of Shull, Woodard went on a speaking tour with the NAACP to make a push for civil rights gains. During one particular speech, he told the crowd, "Negro veterans that fought in the war do not realize that the real battle has just begun in America." This speech would become a rallying call and echo well into the 1960s as the civil rights movement gained steam among World War II veterans.

The aftermath of the state probe also affected how the FBI worked with New York State civil rights groups. Operating in the shadows, the FBI expanded its surveillance into several activists involved in demanding justice for the Ferguson brothers. FBI reports cited Stanley Faulkner, the Ferguson family lawyer connected to the Communist Party and the *Daily Worker* publication, who allegedly used the NAACP as a potential vector for spreading communist ideals. The FBI focused on local links to the NAACP and Faulkner/leftist groups that were established in the days following the shooting of Charles and Alphonso Ferguson. Understanding how its goals could be compromised by being associated with communist-affiliated groups, the NAACP locally denounced communism. Despite the NAACP attempting to distance itself from suspected communists, the FBI in 1950 had informants attending daily NAACP meetings in Nassau and Suffolk Counties to assess the potential

Isaac Woodard, applying for maximum disability benefits, seated with David Edwards. Standing are (*left to right*) Oliver W. Harrington, Edward Nottage, and his mother, Mrs. Isaac Woodard. *Courtesy of the Library of Congress.*

connection to communist groups. In the FBI report, informants stated that "American Labor Party members are active in the NAACP branches of Suffolk and Nassau Counties and could redirect the activities of the local NAACP chapters. The American Labor Party had directed labor unions to communist control for years."[132] In the coming decade, the NAACP would further distance itself from long-standing allied leftist groups associated with communism. At its national convention, the NAACP extended a resolution that banned members with communist affiliation. Another anticommunist method rolled out was picking and choosing individuals to defend.

An example of a civil rights case for which the NAACP provided limited assistance came on July 23, 1948, with the police shooting death of mechanic Willies Milton in Williamsburg, Brooklyn. Milton was believed to be radicalized from the Ferguson case and a member of a communist-affiliated group. On July 23, Milton argued in a local bar over the tab. The argument escalated, and rookie officer Peter Kilcommons came into the bar to break up the fight, which resulted in the bartender and Milton hurling glasses. The officer then took out his gun, and as Milton ran out of the bar down Bedford Avenue, the officer shot and killed him. Following her husband's death, Irene Milton told the press, "I don't want Georgia to Come to New York [Irene was giving an indirect reference to the *Daily Worker* publication "Dixie Comes to New York"]. I will fight this case to the end."[133] Leading the charge for justice was Dorothy Langston, an executive secretary for the Committee for Justice. Langston was the leader of the Committee for Ferguson Brothers Justice and connected to communist-affiliated groups. Like Freeport in 1946, the *Daily Worker* published a pamphlet detailing the shooting titled "A Lynch Tree Grows in Brooklyn." Unlike the Ferguson case, the NAACP distanced itself from the Milton case as communist and leftist groups became involved.

The Civil Rights Congress (CRC) picked up the calls for justice in the aftermath of the Ferguson brothers and Milton shootings. Similar to years prior, with local groups demanding justice, the CRC's demands for justice became silenced due to having members associated with the Communist Party. Founder William Patterson was a civil rights lawyer and head of the International Labor Defense, which focused on legal issues relating to the Communist Party. In 1951, the CRC wrote the petition "We Charge Genocide" to be presented at the December 1951 Paris United Nations annual meeting. The petition argued that the United States violated the UN Genocide Convention of 1948, Article II—"killing, causing mental and severe bodily harm to members of a racial, ethnic or religious group." Detailed was the white supremacy that enforced a lower quality of life for Black citizens. But racially motivated violence and lynchings from 1945 to 1951 in the United States were highlighted with the most graphic detail. On page 61, it read:

> *A policeman of Freeport, L.I., New York, shot and killed PFC. Charles Ferguson and his brother, Alphonso Ferguson. A third brother, Seaman Third Class Joseph Ferguson, was wounded. While a fourth brother, Richard Ferguson, was arrested and sentenced to 100 days in jail. The brothers had protested Jim Crow at a local cafe, where the proprietor had refused them service because they were Negroes. The Chief of Police and the Nassau Grand Jury acquitted the killer-policeman. After five months of organized protest, an investigation ordered by Governor Dewey whitewashed the police and the grand jury, which refused to indict the policeman and the District*

> *Attorney of Nassau County. The investigation also denied the lawyer for the slain brothers' families the right to cross-examination and the right to put specific questions to witnesses.*[134]

Copies of the petition were made and circulated within the New York United Nations by African American singer Paul Robeson with Amy Mallard and Josephine Gray, both widowed from a lynching. Robeson attempted to get a passport to present the petition in Paris with CRC, but the state department denied him.[135] William L. Patterson distributed the petition among the delegates in Paris. Before he met with the delegates, Patterson got a call from the state department at his hotel demanding that he surrender his passport. Patterson refused the demands and had his passport confiscated upon his return to New York by government officials.[136] In response to the efforts of CRC, one of the authors of the Genocide Convention, Raphael Lemkin, asserted that "communist sympathizers are falsely accusing the United States of genocide in an attempt to divert the UN from true genocidal crimes of the Soviet Union. These [crimes listed in the petition] may be unjust and discriminatory, but they are not intended to destroy the colored race. Existence on a lower level is not the same as non-existence."[137] Despite the setback at the United Nations, gains were made in a series of U.S. Supreme Court rulings. The 1948 Supreme Court case *Shelley v. Kraemer* would draw the battle lines for civil rights gains and fights in the decades to come. The decision ruled that racially restrictive covenants in housing violated the Fourteenth Amendment's equal protection clause. Challenging this ruling nationwide would be Long Island–based developer Levitt and Sons.

Levitt and Sons constructed its postwar suburbia on over one thousand acres of former potato fields referred to as Island Trees. More than 17,447 Cape Cod homes were built at 36 houses daily to feed the growing demand for housing. Each home was eight hundred square feet, on concrete slabs, with a washer, dryer, built-in television, modern kitchen appliances, and an optional carport. In 1944, Congress passed the Servicemen's Readjustment Act, referred to as the G.I. Bill. The bill provided low-interest mortgages with no money down. The original loan amount guaranteed under the bill was $4,000, but due to inflation and the increased prices of building a house, the guaranteed loan amount was increased to $8,000. Levitt advertised newly built homes for under $8,000, with veteran preference in accepting and processing applications. All media publications throughout the tristate area targeted the 900,000

Returning Black soldiers in New York celebrating victory in Japan. *Courtesy of New York Public Library.*

New York State veterans by selling the idea of an affordable garden community. The parkways system connecting Nassau County to Queens, Brooklyn, and Manhattan made the development more marketable.

Left out in these advertisements was that only white veterans were desired. Levitt and Sons barred Black families from renting their homes and steered them away from buying their homes. Levitt and Sons' reluctant allies included local banks that refused to provide or process VA mortgages to Black families seeking houses in Levitt developments.[138] Before purchasing a Levitt house, many prospective buyers rented the home with the option of buying. Homeowners had to agree to clause 26 within the rental agreement: "The tenant agrees not to permit the premises to be used or occupied by any person other than members of the Caucasian race, but the employment and maintenance of other than Caucasian domestic servants shall be permitted." This clause was enforced through evictions and steep fines to the landlords if privately owned. In the early years of Levittown, the clause was used against residents whose children played in interracial groups within the community. Many postwar Long Island banks retained relics of the 1920s Klan. Paul Lindner, the

Eugene Burnett and Richard Coles returning home following their discharge. *Courtesy of Eugene Burnett.*

developer who built the community of Malvern just west of Island Trees/ Levittown, formed various home lending companies. Lindner, in 1927, also held the rank of Great Titan of the New York State Klan. In this role, Lindner managed the various Nassau County Klan chapters. John Boyle Jr. was the vice president of one of Long Island's first and most prominent mortgage companies, the Homeland Corporation. Boyle, like Lindner, held a high rank in the 1920s Long Island Klan. During the development of Levittown, both Boyle and Lindner were technically out of the lending business, but the companies they founded kept many of the lending policies they created in effect for decades.

Lending institutions' racial ideologies and Levitt racial clauses were rebranded not as racism but as an economic argument through real estate values. Redlining banks, racial clauses, and racial steering marketed to middle-class white homeowners were rationalized as ways to preserve home values. These race-based real estate policies directly violated the Supreme Court ruling in *Shelley v. Kraemer*. This ruling banned any funds provided by the Federal Housing Administration, which was the bulk funding of all mortgages throughout the country, but loans were underwritten locally. The biases of locals who processed loans became Levitt and Sons' argument for their racial policies. Racial restrictions, lack of enforcement of anti-discrimination laws, and the influx in population disparity across Long Island would be just some of the factors that gained prominence in the second civil rights movement. Nationally, an estimated 1.2 million Black citizens served during World War II, with the guiding idea that they were ending tyranny and promised a path to the middle class through the G.I. Bill and a guaranteed no-money-down VA mortgage. Upon returning home, these citizens and their families, all over the country

JOB NO. 1574

Lease dated January 21st, 1948, between LEVITTOWN CORPORATION ~~ISLAND TREES CORP.~~, a New York Corporation, located at 3230 Northern Boulevard, Manhasset, New York, as Landlord, and Herbert Cantor, residing at 170 E. Broadway, Long Beach, New York, as Tenant.

The Landlord leases to the Tenant premises at Island Trees, Hicksville, N. Y., known by street number as 41 Lilac Lane for a term commencing on February 1st, 1948, and expiring on January 31st, 1949, for residential occupancy by the Tenant and the Tenant's immediate family upon the following conditions and covenants:

1. The Tenant agrees to pay rent at the annual rate of $720.00, payable $60.00 monthly in advance on the first day of each month.

2. The Tenant agrees to take good care of the premises and of the household equipment furnished therewith, and forthwith at the Tenant's expense to make all repairs thereto not necessitated by the Landlord's fault, except that the Landlord, at its expense, will make all major structural repairs to the premises not necessitated by the Tenant's fault or that of the Tenant's family, employees, invitees or licensees. The Tenant agrees to deliver up the premises and equipment in good condition at the expiration of the term.

3. The Tenant agrees not to assign this lease or underlet the premises or any part thereof.

4. The Tenant agrees to allow the Landlord to enter the premises at all reasonable hours to examine the same or make repairs.

5. The Tenant agrees that the Landlord shall be exempt from liability for any damage or injury to person or property except such as may be caused by its negligence.

6. The Tenant agrees that this lease shall be subordinate to any mortgages now or hereafter on the premises.

7. The Tenant agrees to comply with all of the statutes, ordinances, rules, orders, regulations and requirements of the Federal, State and Municipal Governments, Departments and Bureaus, applicable to the premises.

8. The Tenant agrees not to do, bring or keep or to permit to be done, brought or kept on the premises anything which will in any way increase the rate of fire insurance thereon.

9. THE TENANT HAS DEPOSITED WITH THE LANDLORD THE SUM OF $100.00 AS SECURITY FOR THE PERFORMANCE OF THIS LEASE, WHICH SUM WITHOUT INTEREST SHALL BE RETURNED TO THE TENANT AFTER THE EXPIRATION OF THE TERM HEREIN PROVIDED THE TENANT HAS FULLY PERFORMED. THE TENANT AGREES NOT TO ASSIGN OR ENCUMBER THE SECURITY.

10. The Tenant agrees that the failure of the Landlord to insist upon a strict performance of any of the conditions and covenants herein shall not be deemed a waiver of any rights or remedies that the Landlord may have, and shall not be deemed a waiver of any subsequent breach or default in the conditions and covenants herein contained. This instrument may not be changed, modified or discharged orally.

11. The Tenant agrees that should the premises or any part thereof be condemned for public use, this lease, at the option of the Landlord, shall become null and void upon the date of taking and rent shall be apportioned as of such date. No part of any award, however, shall belong to the Tenant.

12. The Tenant agrees that if, upon the expiration of the term, the Tenant fails to remove any property belonging to the Tenant, such property shall be deemed abandoned by the Tenant and shall become the property of the Landlord.

13. The Tenant agrees to waive all rights to trial by jury in any summary proceedings hereafter instituted by the Landlord against the Tenant in respect to the premises or in any action brought to recover rent or damages hereunder.

14. The Tenant agrees that the obligation of the Tenant to pay rent and perform all of the other conditions and covenants hereof shall not be affected by the Landlord's inability, because of circumstances beyond its control, to supply any service or to make any repairs or to supply any equipment or fixtures.

15. The Tenant agrees to employ and pay the garbage and rubbish collector designated by the Landlord, in default of which the Landlord may make such payment and charge the same to the Tenant as additional rent.

16. The Tenant agrees that the premises are being rented "as is" and that the Landlord shall not be obligated to make any alterations, improvements or renovations therein, nor any repairs other than those expressly provided for herein.

17. THE TENANT AGREES TO ASSUME THE RESPONSIBILITY OF ENSURING THAT NO PERSON SHALL WALK AND NOTHING SHALL BE PLACED UPON THE UNFINISHED SECTION OF THE ATTIC FLOOR AND THAT IN THE EVENT THIS CONDITION IS VIOLATED AND DAMAGE RESULTS TO SUCH ATTIC FLOOR AND/OR TO THE CEILING BELOW, THE TENANT WILL PAY UPON DEMAND AS ADDITIONAL RENT THE COST OF REPAIRS WHICH ARE ESTIMATED AT A MINIMUM OF $60.00.

18. The Tenant agrees that the Landlord assumes no obligation for the servicing or repair of the oil burner, washing machine, cooking stove, refrigerator, or ventilating fan installed in the premises. Solely for the convenience of the Tenant, the Landlord has made the following arrangements, for the carrying out of which, however, the Landlord shall not be held responsible:

> The oil burner parts are represented by the manufacturer as guaranteed for one year.
>
> If and so long as the Tenant purchases fuel oil from Live Heat, Inc., it is represented by that Company that the oil burner will be serviced without charge.
>
> Bruno-New York, Inc., represents that the washing machine will be serviced without charge for one year.
>
> The manufacturer of the cooking stove represents that its parts are guaranteed for one year but no service is to be provided.
>
> The manufacturer of the refrigerator represents that it will be serviced for one year.
>
> The ventilator is not guaranteed at all nor will there be any servicing of it.

19. The Landlord will furnish at its own expense water consumed on the premises in reasonable quantities for ordinary domestic and gardening purposes.

20. The Tenant agrees not to erect or permit to be erected any fence, either fabricated or growing, upon any part of the premises.

21. The Tenant agrees not to keep or permit to be kept any animals, pigeons or fowl upon the permises except not more than two domestic animal pets.

22. The Tenant agrees not to install or permit to be installed any laundry poles or lines outside of the house, except that one portable revolving laundry dryer, not more than seven feet high, may be used in the rear yard on days other than Saturdays, Sundays and legal holidays, provided that such dryer shall be removed from the outside when not in actual use on such permitted days.

23. The Tenant agrees not to place or permit to be placed any garbage or rubbish outside of the house except in a closed metal receptacle located to the rear of the kitchen door and not more than one foot from the exterior of the house and except when placed at the curbline before removal in accordance with the regulations of the collecting agency.

24. THE TENANT AGREES NOT TO RUN OR PARK OR PERMIT TO BE RUN OR PARKED ANY MOTOR VEHICLE UPON ANY PART OF THE PREMISES.

LEVITTOWN HISTORY COLLECTION

25. THE TENANT AGREES TO CUT OR CAUSE TO BE CUT THE LAWN AND REMOVE OR CAUSE TO BE REMOVED TALL GROWING WEEDS AT LEAST ONCE A WEEK BETWEEN APRIL FIFTEENTH AND NOVEMBER FIFTEENTH IN EACH YEAR. UPON THE TENANT'S FAILURE THE LANDLORD MAY DO SO AND CHARGE THE COST THEREOF TO THE TENANT AS ADDITIONAL RENT.

26. THE TENANT AGREES NOT TO PERMIT THE PREMISES TO BE USED OR OCCUPIED BY ANY PERSON OTHER THAN MEMBERS OF THE CAUCASIAN RACE BUT THE EMPLOYMENT AND MAINTENANCE OF OTHER THAN CAUCASIAN DOMESTIC SERVANTS SHALL BE PERMITTED.

27. The Tenant agrees not to place or permit to be placed upon the premises any sign whatsoever except a family or professional name or address plate whose size, style and location are first approved in writing by the Landlord.

28. The Terant agrees not to use or permit the premises to be used for any purpose other than as a private dwelling for one family or as a professional office of a physician or dentist resident therein.

29. The Tenant agrees not to erect or permit to be erected on the premises any building or structure, or to make or permit to be made any alterations or additions to the premises, or paint or permit to be painted the exterior of the house other than in the original color, unless appropriate plans, specifications and/or colors are first approved in writing by the landlord.

30. The Tenant agrees not to do or permit to be done on the premises anything of a disreputable nature, or constituting a nuisance, or tending to impair the condition or appearance of the premises, or tending to interfere unreasonably with the use and enjoyment of other premises by other Tenants, [redacted]

31. The Tenant agrees that, if default be made in the performance of any of the conditions or covenants herein, or if the premises shall become vacant or if the Tenant shall file a petition in bankruptcy or be adjudicated a bankrupt or make an assignment for the benefit of creditors, the Landlord may (A) re-enter the premises by force, summary proceedings or otherwise, and remove all persons therefrom, without being liable to prosecution therefor, and the Tenant hereby expressly waives the service of any notice in writing of intention to re-enter, or (B) the Landlord may terminate this lease on giving to the Tenant 5 days' notice in writing of its intention so to do, and this lease shall expire on the date fixed for the expiration hereof. Such notice may be given by mail to the Tenant addressed to the premises. The Tenant agrees, in either event, to pay at the same times as the rent is payable hereunder a sum equivalent to such rent; and the Landlord may rent the premises on behalf of the Tenant, (for a period of time beyond the original expiration date of this lease, if it so elects), without releasing the Tenant from any liability, applying any moneys collected, first to the expense of resuming or obtaining possession, second to the restoration of the premises to a rentable condition, and then to the payment of the rent and all other charges due and to become due to the Landlord, any surplus to be paid to the Tenant who shall remain liable for any deficiency.

32. The Landlord agrees that the Tenant on performing the conditions and covenants aforesaid shall and may peacefully and quietly have, hold and enjoy the premises for the term aforesaid.

33. It is mutually agreed that the conditions and covenants contained in this lease shall be binding upon the parties hereto and upon their respective successors, heirs, executors, administrators and assigns.

IN WITNESS WHEREOF, the Landlord has caused these presents to be signed by its proper corporate officer and caused its proper corporate seal to be hereto affixed and the Tenant has hereunto set his hand and seal.

LEVITTOWN CORPORATION
XXXXXXXXXXXXXXCORP.

By: .... Authorized Officer

.... L. S.

NO NOTICES WILL BE MAILED. RENT IS DUE AND PAYABLE ON THE FIRST OF EACH MONTH AT THE OFFICE IN THE ISLAND TREES COMMUNITY.

Opposite and above: Prospective buyers in Levitt developments renting homes with the option to buy had to agree on clause 26 within the lease, which stated, "The tenant agrees not to permit the premises to be used or occupied by any person other than members of the Caucasian race, but the employment and maintenance of other than Caucasian domestic servants shall be permitted." *Courtesy of Levittown Library.*

and on Long Island, found the same conditions they endured before World War II; in some cases, things were worse. Fighting tyranny abroad did not extend to ending racial oppression at home, even after the world witnessed the after-effects of state-sanctioned killings of ethnic minorities throughout Asia and Europe. Returning Black troops demanded the same opportunities as the returning white soldiers. They argued that the American dream was not reserved or owned by a specific race. Mortgage lending, quality schools, fair/equal employment, and anything that would provide a pathway to the middle class were Black veterans' collective desires for the second civil rights movement.

Donald Archer and his mother, Myrtle Archer of Jamaica, Queens, tried buying a house in Levittown in early 1953. Donald, a Black veteran, would have been approved for any VA loan and had the qualified income.[139] When going into the sales office, they were told that "they are not selling to Negros at this time." In an interview with *Newsday* relating to Donald Archer's attempt to buy a Levitt house, a spokesperson for Levittown stated, "Our policy as to whom we sell or do not sell is the same as that of any other builder, in the entire Metropolitan area." Most local '50s and '60s civil rights leaders were Black World War II veterans, rejected from buying homes in Levittown. One example is community activist Eugene Burnett. After receiving his honorable discharge from the U.S. Army, Burnett became one of the first Black Babylon town police officers. Later, the Babylon Police Department would merge with the Suffolk police. Following the department merger, Burnett broke racial boundaries again by becoming the first Black sergeant in the Suffolk County Police force. While moving his family from New York City to Long Island, Burnett and his wife went to Levittown to see a home. The salesman told them, "Levitt and Sons Corp is not selling to Negros now." Not being able to use the benefits of his G.I. Bill due to racism after fighting racism and tyranny abroad motivated him to become a leader in the NAACP. Irwin Quintyne, like Burnett, was honorably discharged from the U.S. Army. And like Burnett, he was told by Levittown sales managers the same story. This encounter mobilized Quintyne to become a leader in the Congress of Racial Equality (CORE).

While mobilization of civil rights groups took shape, the editorial board of *Newsday*, which extensively covered the Ferguson case and other civil rights struggles, remained silent regarding Levitt and Sons Development Corporation. The silence was due to Alicia Patterson, founder of *Newsday*, advocating for expanding low-cost Levitt housing for returning veterans

Eugene Burnett was the first Black sergeant in the Suffolk County police force. *Courtesy of Eugene Burnett.*

at all costs. In a *Newsday* podcast series, journalist Mark Chiusano stated, "Patterson believed William Levitt was what Long Island needed. She campaigned to eliminate any building code that will conflict with a Levitt development, which also included any challenge against racial discrimination of housing."[140] When discrimination cases or protests were covered, it would be a small paragraph tucked away from the headline pages in the center of the paper.

The racial clause in Levittown was challenged in court by Black veteran William Cotter. He was evicted from Levittown in 1953 after a white friend signed the lease for him and his family. After taking his case to the highest level of the state Supreme Court, he was permitted to rent and later buy a home in the development by 1959. While the state courts ruled in favor of William Cotter, CORE became ingrained as a force protesting against housing discrimination. Like decades prior in the Ferguson case, local officials underplayed the racial disparities and labeled activists as communist agitators.

COMMITTEE TO END DISCRIMINATION IN LEVITTOWN 1951

POST OFFICE BOX 53, LEVITTOWN, LONG ISLAND, N. Y.

Dear Friend:

The Constitution says "yes"...The Supreme Court says "yes"...But William Levitt and Sons say "no."

By openly refusing to rent or sell homes to Negroes, the Levitt organization has run counter to American democratic thought, and has condemned Levittown in the eyes of all thinking Americans who believe that now, as never before, the fullest expression of democracy is mandatory.

Two years ago, our Committee was formed to halt Levitt's discriminatory practices. As a result of our joint action with groups like American Veterans' Committee, National Association for the Advancement of Colored People, American Civil Liberties Union and others, Levitt was forced to remove a restrictive covenant clause from his contracts. We have prevented, thus far, Levitt's attempted eviction of families who entertained Negro children in their homes...We have welcomed and helped successfully absorb into Levittown life the first Negro family to rent a house from a private owner...We have energetically publicized through the press, door-to-door visits and public meetings our Committee's efforts to end discrimination.

Community response to our program convinces us that Levittown sincerely believes in democracy. Nevertheless, we have not yet compelled Levitt and Sons to practice it...What remains for us to do? What final steps must we take? This is the urgent question we are now posing to hundreds of responsible organizations and individuals ...Will you, personally, or with your organization, join us in sponsoring a non-partisan, non-political Conference to find an answer to this problem? Will you participate in a Conference to focus public opinion on Levitt's dangerous practices?

We have scheduled this Conference for Thursday evening, June 7, at Hofstra College in Hempstead. Since we are eager to prepare our official Conference Call, will you tell us as soon as you can of your sponsorship and participation?

Help us realize Levittown's boast as "the Veterans' paradise - for all." Write to us - now.

Sincerely yours,

COMMITTEE TO END DISCRIMINATION

William G. Cotter

William G. Cotter, Chairman

Local residents in Levittown who supported William Cotter formed the Committee to End Discrimination. *Courtesy of Levittown Library.*

Civil rights organizations, such as the Levittown-Wantagh Committee for Brotherhood, were publicly denounced as communists and were blocked from speaking at any community forums within Levittown. Like activists in the Ferguson justice campaigns, they were banned from local

Elks Club Halls. This committee of seventy to two hundred people drew attention through its Operation Suburbia plan, which had local volunteers host inner-city minority kids for summer to enjoy the amenities of Nassau County.[141] These events came with solid resistance from locals. Intimidation toward the CORE, Levittown-Wantagh Committee for Brotherhood, and other civil rights groups was done through the Society for the Prevention of Negroes Getting Everything (SPONGE). SPONGE comprised local youths who were Barry Goldwater supporters, anticommunists, and anti-integrationists. SPONGE was embedded within the Levittown, Hicksville, and East Meadow communities but originated in New York City's white working-class neighborhoods, which protested new families of color moving in by picketing or bullying the new residents.[142] On Long Island, SPONGE counter-protested all CORE demonstrations and disrupted civil rights demonstrations through bomb threats or starting fights with activists. One example was a CORE demonstration of five hundred people protesting housing discrimination at Vigilant Associates in Hicksville. At the rally, SPONGE counter-protested by carrying Confederate flags and holding signs of support for Barry Goldwater, with racial slurs comparing CORE to communist agitators. The counter-protests would later evolve into fights, where bottles and other objects were thrown at CORE members. The aggression from SPONGE undermined the campaign goals of CORE by forcing the police to break up the event for safety reasons. Other prominent anti-integration groups included the Taxpayers and Parents Association. This group generated a misinformation campaign against school and community integration and masked its racist reasoning through economics—it argued that integrated schools led to lower standards and reduced property values. This misinformation constructed a more stigmatized label for people of color and further escalated racial tensions.

Civil rights across Long Island took a back seat regardless of the efforts of CORE and the local NAACP chapters. Politically, these sentiments were reflected in the 1964 presidential elections. Republican candidate Barry Goldwater vehemently opposed the Civil Rights Act and made his opposition a part of his domestic agenda. The results of the 1964 election were that Johnson won the popular vote in Suffolk and Nassau Counties but with a slim margin of just over 50 percent of the vote. Civil rights not being front and center in the development of postwar Nassau and Suffolk Counties led to issues of equality and equity persisting for decades. For example, within the 124 local school districts throughout the island, funding was based on local tax revenues from residential and

Taxpayers And Parents asso.

P. O. BOX 231
MALVERNE, NEW YORK

October 27, 1965

Dear Neighbor,

Since it involves your home and children I am sure you know that the Supreme Court has refused to listen to our appeal. This means that Commissioner Allen has the power to force us to adopt the Princeton Plan, as he ordered us to do over two years ago.

Of course the plan will fail. But it will do more than just fail--it will destroy the presently integrated Malverne School District and create in its place, a "resegregated" school district.

Acting Supt said Plan will succeed

A "resegregated" district is one that has passed from being predominately white to being predominately Negro.

In the last three years the very threat of the Princeton Plan has changed Malvern School District #12 dramatically.

Now more than 50% of the pupils in the combined lower grades and Junior High School are Negro--and that percentage grows day by day.

Acting Supt Said Not So

Only the prospect of the institution of the Princeton Plan was enough to cause white people with children of school age, with rare exception, to refuse to move into our district, (unless their children were expected to go to private schools). Look around you--see what kind of families move out of our school district,--and see what kind move in. The normal replacement of older families with grown children by younger families with school-age children is simply not taking place.

Acting Supt Said Not So

Even though not a single Negro family has moved into the Lynbrook or Malverne sections of our school district and white adults outnumber Negro adults more than two to one, Negro children have become the majority in our schools! And the percentage grows day by day!

Unless the threat of the Princeton Plan is removed forthwith this trend will continue, until a white child in the public schools will be an oddity.

Parents simply will not tolerate their children being bussed out of their neighborhoods involuntarily!

Commissioner Allen found that out in New York City when white children "evaporated" from his "integrated" bussed Princeton Plan School districts.

No court can prevent white parents from moving out of school districts, nor Negro parents from moving in. While lawyers were arguing and judges deliberating that's just what has been happening in Malverne School District #12. But, once the Princeton Plan is implemented, what has been the wind of change will become a hurricane of destruction. That's how it happened elsewhere and that's what must happen here.

No Negroes live in Malverne

And that is why the Princeton Plan is "dead" in New York City, with NAACP and CORE consent and approval.

But the school areas in New York City on which it was tried are "dead" too--that is, dead to integration, they have become predominately Negro areas.

Must this happen to Malverne School District #12?

Must we become a "resegregated" Negro School District?

Not necessarily.

Not if Commissioner Allen withdraws from backing the Princeton Plan in Malverne, as he withdrew from backing the Princeton Plan in New York City.

And how can this happen? If, in any way, it can be caused by your letters. All you parents and taxpayers, white and Negro, must write Commissioner Allen demanding that he kill the Princeton Plan. If you don't, you will have no one to blame but yourself when you end up with a segregated all Negro Malverne School District #12. The address is:

Dr. James E. Allen, Jr.
Commissioner of Education
State Education Department
Albany, New York

Charles W. Reardon, Pres.
Taxpayers and Parents Association

In response to growing civil rights activism, pro-segregation groups were formed to promote segregation policies. One such group was the Taxpayers and Parent Association, which argued that segregation was an economic necessity. *Courtesy of New York State Historical Archives.*

commercial properties. In non-white areas, the commercial tax base was either nonexistent or compromised by elected officials granting tax abatements to properties, which gave them the option not to pay school taxes if they stayed within the community. In communities of color, the tax base would fall almost exclusively on residential homes, limiting funding to schools of color.

Failing schools affected the resale values of homes, which lowered generational wealth in communities of color. In contrast, white schools enjoyed a broad tax base from commercial districts such as strip malls or industrial plants. These factors paved the way for income inequity and the wealth gap between white communities and communities of color. This disparity became the civil rights front on Long Island that was half a century in the making, becoming a battlefront for the twenty-first century. This was the Long Island that the Ferguson family inherited following the deaths of Charles and Alphonso.

Chapter 12

FREEPORT AND THE FERGUSON FAMILY

Freeport of 1951 changed rapidly in population, political views, and shared memories. In the years after Dewey declared the state probe closed and the public's attention shifted toward justice in the Isaac Woodard case, Freeport attempted to rebrand its police department through community-sponsored events. During the rebranding efforts, Stanley Faulkner filed a lawsuit against the village police for the deaths of Charles and Alphonso and the malicious persecution of Richard. The suit totaled $47,000 in 1947. The following year, the same chargers in the original lawsuit were filed against the Village of Freeport for $50,000 in damages. Both cases would be dismissed. In a final effort, the case was refiled, and in 1951, it was dismissed for the last time. The media did not cover the filing and dismissal of the suit in detail. Local interest shifted, and much of the community seemed to suffer from collective amnesia of the February 5, 1946 events.

One Freeport village police rebranding effort was establishing the Police Boys Club. The club had the original objective of establishing sports teams and providing a safe place to play. Following the club's formation, the department appointed Joseph Romeika to lead the organization's day-to-day management. His appointment came with the endorsement of Freeport American Legion, one of the few American Legion Posts that declared its support for Freeport officials in not indicting Romeika after the shooting. Under Romeika's leadership, the group quickly expanded into fishing trips, model boat building and racing contests, annual baseball games, organized sports teams, and community service. In all local media outlets, Romeika received praise as reporters documented what the club had scheduled and done daily. In a government-funded documentary called *American Way of Life*, a soapbox derby race organized by the club was filmed, which gave him more local coverage. His club received further praise for fundraising for the funeral and burial expenses of an eight-year-old local boy who drowned. Once, a kid approached Romeika over a secret teenage boxing ring. Young underage boys were given fake IDs and paired up to fight semiprofessional boxers in prizefights. Romeika led an investigation, which saw charges filed against E.P.F. Eagan, the chairman of the New York State Boxing Commission. While making headlines for the club's activities and high-profile cases, Romeika also mandated that his Boys Club members denounce communism and pledge not to use "dope" within the club. In one editorial directed at parents in the Freeport community, he wrote:

> *Communists are in the United States using dope* [as a] *strategy to cripple our youth. We have never had such a high rate of youthful addicts in the history of the United States. Never before have we seen so many teenagers sent to hospitals to treat this vicious drug. The Communists are poisoning the minds of our youth in our schools, especially in New York City. Many reputable people are claiming. Communist underground workers have branched out to organize dope peddling to youth—to make them unfit for military service. During the war, the Japanese were effective in an onslaught against the Chinese because the young Communist youths were drug addicts and, therefore, unfit for military service.*[143]

While on his anticommunism crusade and leading the Boys Club, Romeika would mail club applications daily to Charles's children, Charles Jr., Wilfred, and Richard. The application had an events calendar and an invitation to join, with Romeika's address. Minnie would throw the literature out and angrily say, "He has some nerve."[144] In most communities of color in Freeport, Black children did not sign up for the Boys Club due to the lasting effects of 1920s Klan influence in the village and the Ferguson shootings. This not too far distant history cemented a generational legacy of distrust among the populations of color and the village law enforcement.

In the early 1950s, Romeika married Sally Ruth MacMillan of Freeport, but this sense of normalcy was only a façade. Romeika was an alcoholic, and it was unclear how long he had been hiding the problem. By April 1954, due to the craving for the spotlight in local media and his crippling drinking problem, Romeika was removed and reassigned as a patrol officer by the Freeport police chief. While on duty, Romeika used to drive to the surrounding town of Merrick to drink for hours and later return to his duties in Freeport to avoid getting caught by local officials. In his later years, Romeika's drinking got worse. By 1962, the Freeport Police Department had hired Julius Pearse, the village's first Black officer, and partnered him up with Romeika. During these years, Pearse recalled that Romeika was not a racist person but was constantly drunk and only concerned about his next drink. Romeika was so consumed by alcoholism that Pearse did not even know if he had a family because drinking was his full-time job. Romeika and fellow officer Bob Gordon, the Freeport officers union head, used to drink throughout their shifts and did little to hide it from their peers. During one of his patrols in Freeport, Romeika stopped in a bar and lost his nightstick. He told everyone in the bar that no one would get in trouble if he got it back. He was seen as a joke on the force following the incident. In 1975, all the drinking caught up to Romeika, who passed away.

Charles Jr., Richard, and Wilfred Ferguson would grow up in Roosevelt, their father's legacy and death shaping their adolescence. Minnie would support the family doing domestic work and, in 1958, cashed in a trust created by Dorothy Langston, singer Kenneth Spencer, actress Josephine Premice and director Oskar Homolka via their champagne parties the decade prior. Minnie bought a home for the family in Uniondale with the proceeds. The older surviving brother of Charles and Alphonso, Edward, would move to the D.C. metro area. He kept his family and New York at a distance. Joseph and Richard would make a career of masonry work in the multiple local residential developments. While growing up, brother Richard lived with Minnie. Young Wilfred, up to age six, believed that Richard was his father until he discovered the truth. While Minnie's uncle Bill was visiting the house, he looked at Charles Jr. and said to Minnie, "He looks just like his father, Charles." The remark spurred a conversation that Wilfred was listening to; to his surprise, he learned that his father was killed by Freeport police officer Romeika. After this conversation, the topic was never brought up again within the family. In his later years, Wilfred would hang out with his friends in Bennington Park in a candy and milkshake shop. Among his friends, Wilfred would hear stories of how mean Officer Romeika was, and he quickly became the officer to avoid in his circle of friends. Wilfred and his brothers avoided Officer Romeika during his patrols by timing their visits to occur when he was not on duty. Over the years, Wilfred and his brothers had a frayed relationship with

Left: Joseph Ferguson's grave at Pinelawn Cemetery. *Courtesy of Christopher Verga.*

Below: Ferguson and Gibbons family photo in the early 1990s. *Courtesy of Wilfred Ferguson and Carlo Gibbons.*

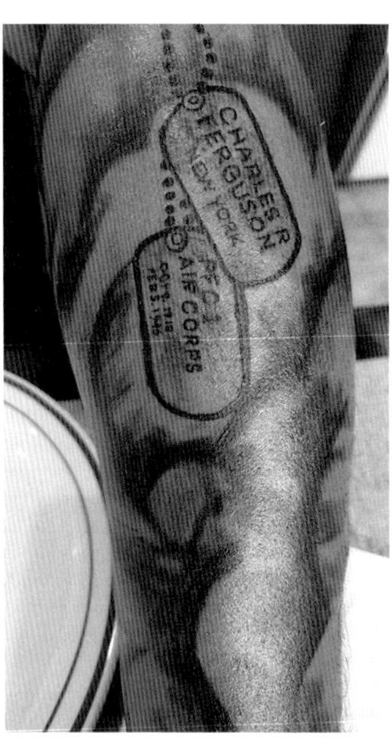

Above: Wilfred Ferguson, son of Charles, being interviewed by News 12 about his father's murder and the unanswered questions. *Courtesy of Wilfred Ferguson and Carlo Gibbons.*

Left: Ferguson family member with Charles's dog tags tattooed on his forearm. *Courtesy of Wilfred Ferguson and Carlo Gibbons.*

their mother, Minnie. When asked about his relationship with his mother in interviews, Wilfred said, "There is not much to say except she was my mother." Wilfred became a mechanic for New York State and settled with his family in Baldwin.

Richard settled in Roosevelt with his family and continued his favorite leisure activity, playing the guitar. Joseph settled on St. Francis Avenue in Roosevelt but died in a house fire in 1971. Both men fathered multiple children and kept the events of February 5, 1946, their biggest family secret to shield their children from knowing their brothers' deaths.

CONCLUSION

After the events that inspired the civil rights movements of the '50s and '60s, the following generation would grow up in their shadow. Notable celebrities who came out to support justice for the Ferguson brothers would revolutionize television programming. Actress Josephine Premice, who organized fundraisers for the Ferguson family and helped mobilize fellow Black Broadway actors and actresses to seek justice for the Ferguson brothers, inspired her daughter Susan False-Hill. The latter went on to upend the racial stereotypes in television by becoming one of the writers on *The Cosby Show* and *A Different World*. These shows changed how Black Americans were portrayed in media. But civil rights struggles of decades past still reverberated into the future locally and nationally.

Echoing the events of February 1946, Nassau County officials and the police department were soon in the headlines for another tragic event. Early Saturday morning on November 28, 1971, the Freeport and Roosevelt community witnessed another shooting death of an unarmed Black person. Police spotted sixteen-year-old Lawrence Blaylock of Freeport in a suspected stolen car, which triggered a police car chase for six miles through the town of Lynbrook to Roosevelt.[145] Blaylock was diagnosed as intellectually disabled. While being chased, Blaylock and his companion ditched the car and started running from the police down Babylon Turnpike in Roosevelt. Toward the end of the block near a wooded area, police with guns drawn yelled at Blaylock and his companion to stop. Blaylock stopped and crouched. His crouching could have been from him being out of breath from the chase, but Nassau County Officer Frank Parisi mistook his posture as him reaching for a gun. Blaylock was shot through the neck and killed by the officer steps away from 93 Bennett Avenue, the Ferguson brothers' home. Like with the shooting death of Charles and Alphonso, the officer was not suspended following the shooting. The jury in the Blaylock murder comprised twenty-two white people and one Black person. Like with the events of 1946, the officer was acquitted of any wrongdoing.

Since Charles, Alphonso, and Blaylock's deaths, the police department has rolled out many reforms, and police forces in multiple villages/counties have seen modest gains in diversity within their rank and file. In 2020, in response to the murder of George Floyd at the hands of police officers in Minneapolis, New York State Governor Andrew Cuomo issued Executive Order 223. This order requested all state police departments create a plan to bridge the gap in community trust and prevent the deaths of unarmed suspects or civilians. The Freeport Police Department published a 163-page plan in April 2021. The plan detailed transparency of police actions in Freeport's community, community-based outreach, and a concise protocol of when (and when not) to use lethal force. The use of deadly force is permitted "to protect him/herself or another person believed to be an imminent threat of serious physical injury or death."[146] Time will judge the effectiveness of these policies.

The most significant shift in reform has come about due to changing demographics. According to the 2020 U.S. Census, Nassau County's population comprises 42 percent minority groups and 58 percent white of no Hispanic/Latino origin. In Suffolk County, the 2020 census reported that the population consists of 34 percent minority groups and 66 percent white of no Hispanic/Latino origins. In Freeport's village, 66 percent of residents are part of a minority group, and 34 percent are white of no Hispanic/Latino origins. By 2009, Freeport had elected its first Black mayor, Andrew Hardwick. Within twelve years of this, the village police department had promoted Michael Williams to become the first Black deputy chief of the department. Inequities throughout Long Island persist in schools, housing, and the justice system, but the overall shift in demographics can potentially have the greatest impact on transforming and solving these problems.

With the advent of social media, a hashtag or a like on Facebook rarely materializes events like the Black Lives Matter protests of 2020. Overall, echoes of the past are silenced through the societal amnesia of a community trying to forget its history. Lack of historical awareness and temporary fixes to appease community outrage create other challenges. Short-term fixes may further the conversation of historical inequalities, but in many cases, they do not leave the dialogue stage and stall any lasting reform. The frustrations of the grieving Ferguson family were spotlighted briefly before falling back into obscurity, potentially dooming us to repeat the past again. This cycle forces us, at least in the short term, to face those echoes of inequity that arise as shouts from generations past to examine our contemporary civil rights struggles and challenges through more than a hashtag or Facebook debate.

NOTES

Chapter 1

1. Donald Crummell and Curtis Addison, interview by Porsha Williams, Freeport Memorial Library, New York, April 15, 2015.

Chapter 2

2. John Strong, "Who Says the Montauk Tribe Is Extinct?: Judge Abel Blackmar's Decision *Wyandank v. Benson*," *Long Island History Journal* 10, no. 1 (Fall 1997): 49.
3. Jack Forbes, *Black Africans & Native Americans: Color, Race and Caste in the Evolution of Red-Black Peoples* (New York: Basil Blackwell, 1988), 8.
4. Sandi Walker-Brewster, "Early Colored School in North Amityville," *Amityville Record*, December 10, 2014, cited from "Annual School Meeting Vote to Abolish Colored School," *Brooklyn Daily Eagle*, August 11, 1895.
5. Judith Kafka, "Racial Integration, White Appropriation, and School Choices: The Demise of the Colored Schools of Late Nineteenth Century Brooklyn," CUNY Academic Works, Baruch College, 2020, 2, https://academicworks.cuny.edu/cgi/viewcontent.cgi?article=2209&context=bb_pubs.
6. "Resisting Arrest Negro Receives Fatal Wound from Policeman Devin," *South Side Signal*, March 13, 1913, 1.

41. Charles Dryden, interview, Atlanta, Georgia Library of Congress, American Folklife Center, Veterans History Project, November 6, 2001.
42. Conn Mike, "Glen Cove WWII Vet Remembers Days in the Air: Tuskegee Airman Recalls World War II," *Long Island Herald*, June 6, 2019, https://www.liherald.com/stories/glen-cove-wwii-vet-remembers-days-in-the-air,115432?.
43. "Nassau's Fighting Sons Help Speed Country to Victory," *Nassau Daily Review Star*, June 29, 1943, 8.
44. Fernando Christine, "Army Unveils Memorial for Black Soldier Lynched at Georgia Military Base 80 Years Ago," *USA Today*, August 4, 2021, https://www.usatoday.com/story/news/nation/2021/08/04/us-army-memorial-fort-benning-lynched-black-soldier/5482634001.
45. Verga, *World War II Long Island*, 67.
46. Ibid.

Chapter 7

47. Thompson James, "Should I Sacrifice to Live Half American?," *Pittsburgh Courier*, January 31, 1942, 14.
48. Louis Henry Gates, "What Was Black America's Double War?," PBS, 2013, https://www.pbs.org/wnet/african-americans-many-rivers-to-cross/history/what-was-black-americas-double-war.
49. Villard Oswald, "Villard Says: The Negro Militant," *Newsday* (August 4, 1942): 12.
50. C.A. Simmons, *The African American Press: A History of News Coverage during National Crises, with Special Reference to Four Black Newspapers, 1827–1965* (Jefferson, NC: McFarland, 2006), 80, https://books.google.com.
51. Gates, "What Was Black America's Double War?"
52. "Black Labor," *New York Amsterdam News*, December 7, 1940, 16.
53. "Governor Lehman Appoints Mixed Committee to Fight Job Jim Crow," *New York Amsterdam Star-News*, April 5, 1941, 4.
54. Julius Adams, "New York State FEPC Bills Hailed Progress Milestone," *New York Amsterdam News*, December 9, 1944, 15.
55. Dan Burley, "Lieut. Gov Outlines Fights Against Discrimination in New York State," *New York Amsterdam News*, October 10, 1942, 2.
56. John Strausbaugh, *Victory City* (New York: Twelve Illustrated, 2018), 306.
57. Verga, *World War II Long Island*, 64.

58. Ibid., 65.
59. Ibid., 66.
60. Terry Lichtash, "Ives-Quinn Act: The Law Against Discrimination," *St. John's Law Review* 19, no. 2 (April 1945): 170.
61. "Emotions Before Laws," *Newsday* (June 8, 1945): 7.
62. "Anti-Bias Enforcement Begins," *Newsday* (June 29, 1945): 1.
63. Leo Hanning, "First Nassau Test for Civil Rights Law in Court," *Newsday* (February 1, 1946): 3.

Chapter 8

64. Martha Biondi, *To Stand and Fight: The Struggle for Civil Rights in Post War New York City* (Cambridge, MA: Harvard University Press, 2006), 61.
65. Harry Raymond, "Dixie Comes to New York: Story of the Freeport GI Slayings," *Daily Worker*, 1946, 7, https://digital.library.pitt.edu/islandora/object/pitt%3A31735058194105.
66. Public papers of Governor Dewey, "Matter of the Shooting and Death of Charles and Alphonso Ferguson in Nassau County by Joseph Romeika a Village Policeman of the Village of Freeport," witnesses testimonies, February 12, 1946, 426.
67. Raymond, "Dixie Comes to New York," 5.
68. Memorandum, from Assistant Attorney General Theron to New York Director of the FBI, Joseph Romeika, Charles, Richard, Joseph, and Alphonso Ferguson, Civil Rights, April 3, 1946, 5, via FBI Records—The Vault, https://vault.fbi.gov.
69. Ibid., 7.
70. Ibid., 8.
71. Ibid., 10.
72. Ibid., 14.
73. Ibid.
74. Lawrence Greenbaum, Report to Governor Thomas Dewey of the State of New York, on investigation of the Freeport Ferguson, testimony of Peter Elar, July 30, 1946, 227, Dewey Papers, University of Rochester.
75. Public papers of Governor Dewey, Matter of the Shooting and Death of Charles and Alphonso Ferguson, 428.

Chapter 9

76. "Delegation Seeks Probe in Freeport Gun Deaths," *Newsday* (February 7, 1946): 25.
77. Greenbaum Commission into the shooting of the Ferguson brothers in Freeport, hearing transcripts, examination of Stanley Faulkner, 443, July 23, 1946, University of Rochester, Dewey Papers.
78. "Protest Meeting Tonight in Shooting, Retrial Sought," *Newsday* (February 8, 1946): 25.
79. "Ferguson Group to Ask for Special Prosecutor," *Newsday* (February 18, 1946): 3.
80. Raymond, "Dixie Comes to New York," 11.
81. Memorandum, from Assistant Attorney General Theron to New York Director of the FBI, 16.
82. Petition requesting appointment of Special Prosecutor, in the Matter of the Shooting Deaths of Charles and Alphonso Ferguson in Nassau County by Freeport Village Police Officer Joseph Romeika, public papers of Governor Dewey, 1946, 427.
83. "Rabbi Hits Oppression," *Nassau Daily Review-Star*, February 19, 1946, 17.
84. Raymond, "Dixie Comes to New York," 6–7.
85. Minnie Ferguson, letter to Jury Foreman, February 12, 1946, Thomas Dewey Papers, University of Rochester.
86. Helen Dudar, "Jury Clears Cop in Freeport Killings," *Newsday* (February 22, 1946): 1.
87. "Gehrig Supports Action in Slaying, Says Ferguson Case Was Handled Without Any Partiality," *Nassau Daily Review-Star*, March 1, 1946, 26.
88. "Meeting Demands Gehrig Ouster, Probe of Shooting," *Newsday* (February 25, 1946): 30.
89. Biondi, *To Stand and Fight*, 63.
90. Thurgood Marshall, letter to Charles Breitel, February 27, 1946, Thomas Dewey Papers, University of Rochester.
91. Walter White, letter to Thurgood Marshall, February 1946, Thomas Dewey Papers, University of Rochester.
92. Walter White, memo to Thurgood Marshall, February 1946, Thomas Dewey Papers, University of Rochester.
93. Mike Palunbo, "Segregation Racial Hatred and Integration After World War II," 20th Century History Song Book, http://20thcenturyhistorysongbook.com/song-book/race-relations/segregation-racial-hatred-and-integration-after-world-war-ii.

94. Guthrie Woody, Notebook, series 01, number 77, 24, Woody Guthrie Center, https://woodyguthriecenter.org/archives/collections/woody-guthrie-lyrics-collection.
95. Major G.A. Holliday to Lieutenant Col. Weir, Memorandum from Mitchell Field Legal Office, April 15, 1946, New York State Archives, Dewey Papers, Correspondences into the Ferguson Case, NYSA-13682-55, First Term.
96. Grant Reynolds, letter to Charles Breitel, February 27, 1946, Dewey Paper, University of Rochester.
97. "Club Denounces Anti-Romeika Fractions," *Newsday* (March 1, 1946): 25.
98. "Vet Group Head Has No Comment, Says National Chairman Has Adequately Answered Pelgler," *Nassau Daily Review-Star*, March 2, 1946, 14.
99. "Carlino Gives His Data on Shooting Case: No Discrimination Was Found in Study, He Writes Back, Text of Carlino's Letter," *Nassau Daily Review-Star*, March 4, 1946, 17.
100. Ruth Hughes, letter to Governor Dewey, August 7, 1946, New York State Archives, Dewey Papers Correspondences into the Ferguson Case, NYSA-13682-55, First Term, 223.
101. John Purdy, "Hurrah Over Ferguson Case Attributed to Communists," *Nassau Daily Review-Star*, March 11, 1946, 8.
102. "Mayor Fears Strife Bans Ferguson Rally," *Newsday* (March 2, 1946): 3.
103. "Klan Sends Letter to Ferguson Group," *Newsday* (April 9, 1946): 2.
104. "Ferguson Group Asks State Ban KKK," *Newsday* (April 25, 1946): 24.
105. Ben White, "Klan Link Outs State Official: Dewey Fires Officials for KKK Tie," *Newsday* (May 7, 1946): 1.
106. "Kayo KKK," *Newsday* (July 31, 1946): 19.
107. "Ferguson Group Hits Dewey KKK Probe," *Newsday* (May 25, 1946): 5.
108. "Freeport Trust Fund Aids Three Fatherless Kids, Committee Gives Ferguson Children Check for $750," *New York Amsterdam News*, June 29, 1946, 2.
109. "Ferguson Lawyer Winchell Answered," *Newsday* (May 28, 1946): 2.
110. Leo Hanning, "Dessaure Gets 1½ Years in Assault on Cop," *Newsday* (May 17, 1947): 1.
111. "Clergy Reveals Interest in RVC Dessaure Investigation," *Newsday* (June 15, 1946): 5.
112. Public papers of Governor Dewey, Matter of the Shooting and Death of Charles and Alphonso Ferguson in Nassau County by Joseph Romeika a Village Policeman of the Village of Freeport, witnesses testimonies,

February 12, 1946, letter to Governor Dewey from James Gehrig, July 1, 1946, 435.

113. "Ferguson Probe Will Stick to the Facts, *Newsday* (July 8, 1946): 6.

114. Ibid., 3.

115. "Dewey Appoints Special Probe for Ferguson Shooting Case," *Newsday* (July 6, 1946): 2.

Chapter 10

116. "James N. Gehrig Former L.I. Judge," *New York Times*, June 23, 1971, 48.

117. Memorandum, from Assistant Attorney General Theron to New York Director of the FBI, Joseph Romeika, Charles, Richard, Joseph, and Alphonso Ferguson, Civil Rights, April 3, 1946, 1.

118. "Ferguson Case Probe Begun: Want Suggestions, Evidence," *Newsday* (July 12, 1946): 3.

119. "Brothers Describe Freeport Shooting, Two Whose Kin Were Slain by a Policeman Tell of Row in Lunchroom," *New York Times*, July 8, 1946, 27.

120. Public papers of Governor Dewey, Matter of the Shooting and Death of Charles and Alphonso Ferguson in Nassau County by Joseph Romeika a Village Policeman of the Village of Freeport, witnesses testimonies, February 12, 1946, 426.

121. Theodore Curphey, autopsy of Charles and Alphonso Ferguson, February 5, 1946, Nassau County Grand Jury testimony, investigation into the death of Charles and Alphonso Ferguson, Dewey Papers, University of Rochester.

122. Greenbaum Commission, July 15, 1946, testimony from Theodore Curphey, Dewey Papers, University of Rochester, 168.

123. Ibid., 169.

124. "Call Ferguson Probe Whitewash," *Newsday* (July 19, 1946): 16.

125. "Gehrig Slaps Reds in Ferguson Furor, Communists Blamed by Gehrig for Furor in Ferguson Case," *Newsday* (July 24, 1946): 38.

126. "57 Walk Out on Ferguson Probe, Call Session Fraud," *Newsday* (July 24, 1946): 3.

127. "Gehrig Action Is Ferguson Case Upheld," *Newsday* (August 3, 1946): 3.

128. Public papers of Governor Dewey, Matter of the Shooting and Death of Charles and Alphonso Ferguson in Nassau County by Joseph Romeika a Village Policeman of the Village of Freeport, witnesses testimonies, February 12, 1946, 429–30.

129. Paul Lockwood, letter to Governor Dewey, July 27, 1946, New York State Archives, Dewey Papers, Correspondences into the Ferguson Case, NYSA-13682-55, First Term, 173.

Chapter 11

130. Andrew Whalen, "Listen to Orson Welles Denounce Police Brutality Against Black WWII Veterans," *Newsweek*, August 26, 2020, https://www.newsweek.com/listen-orson-welles-isaac-woodard-police-brutality-radio-1527586.
131. Michael Gardner, *Harry Truman and Civil Rights: Moral Courage and Political Risks* (Carbondale: Southern Illinois University Press, 2003), 17–18.
132. FBI investigation into the Annual Convention of the NAACP, New York Chapters of Nassau and Suffolk County, 56, FBI Vault Archives, https://vault.fbi.gov/NAACP/NAACP%20Part%202%20of%208/at_download/file.
133. "Civil Rights Group Score Police Commissioner," *New York Amsterdam News*, August 7, 1948, 20.
134. Civil Rights Congress, "We Charged Genocide," 1951, 61.
135. "Paul Asks Passport to Give UN Report," *Washington Afro-American*, December 15, 1951, 18.
136. James Hicks, "Patterson Charges U.S. Stole His Passport," *Washington Afro-American*, January 29, 1952, 13.
137. "UN Asked to Act Against Genocide in United States," *Washington Afro-American*, December 22, 1951, 19.
138. Christopher Verga, *Cold War Long Island* (Charleston, SC: The History Press, 2021), 20.
139. Ibid., 22.
140. Mark Chiusano and Amanda Fiscima, "Long Island Divided," *Newsday and Levittown*, podcast, chapter 1, November 17, 2019.
141. Carole Ashinaze, "LI. Civil Right Group Spurred on by Critics," *Newsday* (December 4, 1968): 3A.
142. Michael Stern, "Anti-Negro Group Loosely Formed: SPONGE Members Are Whites in Interracial Areas," *New York Times*, July 23, 1966, 8.

Chapter 12

143. Joseph Romeika, "Are Commies Using Dope to Cripple Our Youths? Ask a Youth Leader," *Nassau Review-Star*, February 16, 1952, 6.
144. Wilfred Ferguson, interview by Christopher Verga, Roosevelt, New York, March 23, 2021.

Conclusion

145. Jack Healy, "Boy's Slaying Stirs Community," *The Leader*, Freeport edition, December 2, 1971.
146. Village of Freeport Police Department, New York State Police Reform and Reinvention Collaborative, April 2021, 16.

ABOUT THE AUTHOR

Christopher Verga is an instructor in Long Island history and the foundations of American history at Suffolk Community College and contributes to the online local news sites Greater Babylon, Greater Bay Shore Greater Patchogue, and Fire Island News. His published works include *Civil Rights on Long Island* (Images of America, Arcadia Publishing), *Bay Shore* (Images of America, Arcadia Publishing), *Saving Fire Island from Robert Moses* (The History Press), *World War II Long Island: The Homefront in Nassau and Suffolk*, and *Cold War Long Island* (The History Press). Christopher has a doctorate in education from St. John's University. His dissertation work included studies of Long Island Native Americans and the impact of tribal recognition on their cultural identity.